14870

D0236189

1

ST. JOSEPH'S R.C
MIDDLE SCHOOL
HEXHAM

NORTHUMBERLAND SLS	
3201738171	
Bertrams	16/07/2008
S745.5	£14.99

POP-UP CARDS

Jo F Mathieson

NEW
HOLLAND

Author's acknowledgements

I wish to thank my family for their support and encouragement while I have been working on this book: George for his initial mathematical contributions; my daughter Shahana for her continuous enthusiasm and encouragement, and my son Matthew for his sound advice and handy tips. Without them this book may not have happened – thank you for believing in me, I love you!

First published in 2008 by New Holland Publishers (UK) Ltd

London • Cape Town • Sydney • Auckland

Garfield House

86–88 Edgware Road

London W2 2EA

United Kingdom

www.newhollandpublishers.com

80 McKenzie Street

Cape Town 8001

South Africa

Unit 1, 66 Gibbes Street

Chatswood, NSW 2067

Australia

218 Lake Road

Northcote, Auckland

New Zealand

Copyright © 2008 text and designs: Jo F Mathieson

Copyright © 2008 photographs: New Holland Publishers (UK) Ltd

Copyright © 2008 New Holland Publishers (UK) Ltd

Jo F Mathieson has asserted her moral right to be identified as the author of this work.

All rights reserved. No part of this publication may be reproduced, stored in a retrieval system, or transmitted in any form or by any means, electronic, mechanical, photocopying, recording or otherwise, without the prior written permission of the publishers and copyright holders.

ISBN 978 1 84773 076 3

Senior Editor Naomi Waters

Designer Neal Cobourne

Photography Shona Wood

Production Hema Gohil

Editorial Direction Rosemary Wilkinson

1 3 5 7 9 10 8 6 4 2

Reproduction by Pica Digital PTE Ltd, Singapore

Printed and bound by Times Offset, Malaysia

Contents

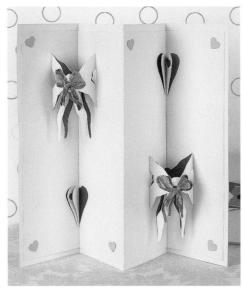

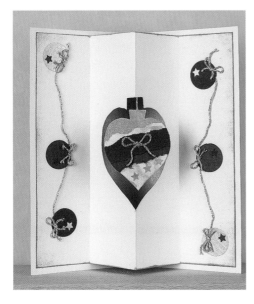

Introduction

Card making embraces a multitude of different ideas, styles and techniques. You are not just creating a great card for family or friends, but also taking the opportunity to let your imagination run wild and "play" with a range of materials and tools. This "craft" promotes creativity in an absorbing and enjoyable way, resulting in a personalized product of which you can be proud!

This book focuses on a long-standing, even historic range of techniques, commonly referred to as a "pop-up", and more technically known as "paper engineering".

Pop-up cards have indeed been around for centuries providing an element of surprise and entertainment, and perhaps had their hey-day in the 19th century. But the question I have always asked myself is how do they work – how can I re-create something similar? Having made many very basic pop-up cards with both adults and children over the past 20 years within a professional capacity, I became more interested in finding out the answer to my question; only to be faced with mathematical calculations, precision drawing and cutting, and a rather full waste-paper basket as a result! Having gone through this process, I have devised simple and easy methods for you to create pop-ups without the frustration. All that's needed is a little patience, and you'll be amazed at the effects that a few simple folds and cuts can create!

The projects in this book have been designed to enable anyone to make a great pop-up card with minimal frustration and maximum enjoyment. Each project is rated:
◆ for beginners to card making and/or pop-ups
◆◆ for intermediate levels of ability
◆◆◆ for those who wish to stretch their skills a little further

The projects cover a wide range of themes and occasions and incorporate a range of basic papercrafting techniques including stamping, embossing, and making simple embellishments. Matching envelopes have been included with some projects and variations have been illustrated on other projects to show you how you can adapt the cards with different colour schemes or for different occasions.

Once you get a feel for pop-ups by working through the simpler projects, you will soon be making all the cards in the book, developing your skills and abilities and getting lots of ideas for new and spectacular designs of your own.

Enjoy making the cards in this book and award yourself the honourable title of "paper engineer"!

Jo xxx
(Now an advanced paper engineer!)

Techniques

A pop-up card has one or several components which, when opened, become mobile and stand forward to create a three-dimensional feature. There are many different techniques that can be adapted to create further dimensions and surprises. The six main techniques used in the projects in this book are explained below.

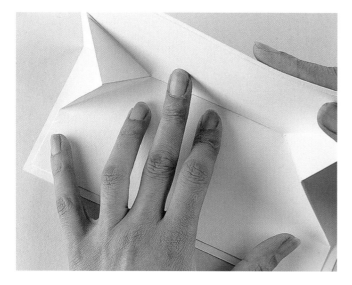

Corner-fold technique

The "corner fold" is a quick and simple technique which creates a platform that allows elements of the overall design to be glued on the sides of the fold and pop forward when opened. The top or bottom centre of the card is pushed forward to create the platform and an outer card is then needed to maintain the shape of the finished card. Both top and bottom corner folds can be used simultaneously to give further interest to the overall design.

Projects using this technique: Easter Chick, New Home, Love Hearts.

Cut-out technique

The cut-out technique requires elements of the design to be partly cut. The cut sections are pushed forward to create the pop-up and the parts intact then act as supports. This technique requires a little practice and a steady hand. An outer card is required to maintain the shape of the finished card.

Projects using this technique: Funny Frog, Wedding Bows.

Sit-up technique

The "sit-up" technique creates a central platform for adding design elements. This technique requires part of the centre fold to be cut and pushed forward. Aspects of the overall design are glued on the front surface of the sit-up section. This technique also requires an outer card to maintain the shape of the finished card.

Projects using this technique: Driving Test, Graduation Day.

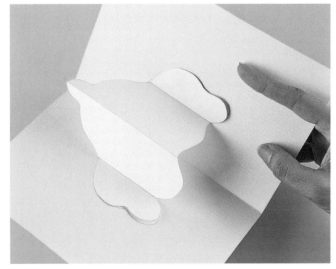

Add-on technique

The add-on technique relies on accurately constructed cubes, prisms or other shapes that can stand forward when folded at the centre. The 'add-on' is glued into a fold on the base card. This technique does not require an outer card as the base card is not cut in any way.

Projects using this technique: Baby Carriage, Birthday Surprise, All Tied Up, Baby Wash Day, Time to Sow.

Panel technique

This technique requires a shaped panel to be created and slits made in the base card into which the panel is inserted to hold it in place. Accurate positioning is required to allow the card to fold easily and an outer card is required to hide the cuts and maintain the shape of the finished card.

Project using this technique: Great News.

Support-tab technique

This technique requires the use of folded tabs to hold a shaped panel in place. Tabs can be various shapes and sizes depending on the overall design. The tabs are glued allowing the pop-up element to sit across the centre fold of the card. No outer card is required.

Project using this technique: Shower of Gifts.

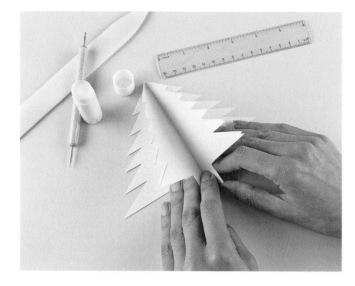

Add-on technique

This technique requires multiple layers of the same shape to be cut and fixed together once folded in the centre. This is then glued into the centre fold of the base card so that when the card is opened the leaves fan out. No outer card is required for this technique.

Project using this technique: Oh Christmas Tree!

Concertina spring technique

Here a piece of the design sits forward on the end of a paper "spring", the other end of which is attached to the base card. The spring is made by sticking the ends of two strips of paper together at 90 degrees, and folding them back and forth over each other; the longer the spring, the greater the movement and "pop-out" effect.

Projects using this technique: Birthday Surprise.

▶ Tying a Bow

This is usually something we are taught as small children. But tying a decorative bow in thin air – as opposed to around a parcel or when pressing against the top of your shoe can stymie lots of people! Follow these simple steps.

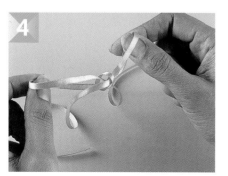

1 Take a length of ribbon, and make a loop in it, with one longer "tail" and one shorter tail.

2 Take the longer tail and wrap it around the base of the loop.

3 Tuck the longer tail, in a loop, under the bit of ribbon that is wrapped around the base of the first loop.

4 Pull the two loops tight to form a bow. Pull tight to the desired size, and trim the tail ends.

▶ Envelopes

The first thing the recipient of a card sees is the envelope. It serves two purposes, primarily, of course, to get the card to the correct postal address in a clean and undamaged condition. However, after all the care and creative effort you will have put into making the very special card it encloses, the envelope can also serve to arouse the anticipation of the recipient. This can be achieved by decorating the envelope in such a way as to give a hint of what lies within.

Decorating envelopes

Decorating envelopes to match the card design enables you to take your ideas one step further and is just as much fun as making the actual card. Anything and everything can be used to decorate an envelope, as long as it is not too heavy or bulky. Choose a particular feature of the design, the colour scheme or the paper and materials used on the card to decorate your envelopes. A few projects in this book (see Shower of Gifts, Wedding Bows and Baby Wash Day) have decorated envelopes that show you the sort of thing that you can achieve.

Making envelopes

With so many ready-made envelopes now available in all sizes, colours and papers, you shouldn't often need to make your own. The basic method is demonstrated on pages 10–11. Some bulkier pop-ups may well need their own custom-made envelope (see template page 110).

The table below shows roughly the measurements of each completed project in this book and the size of paper needed to make an envelope for it. Remember that because pop-up cards can be bulky it is better to buy or make an envelope a little bigger to accommodate the card comfortably.

Project	Dimensions in inches	Dimensions in centimetres	Paper size needed
Baby Carriage	4⅛ × 5¾	10 × 15	210 × 297 mm / 8½ × 11 in
Funny Frog	5⅞ × 8½	14.5 × 21	420 × 297 mm / 11 × 17 in
New Home	5¼ × 5¼	13.5 × 13.5	210 × 297 mm / 8½ × 11 in
Thinking of You	4⅜ × 5¾	10 × 15	210 × 297 mm / 8½ × 11 in
Get Well Soon	5¼ × 5¼	13.5 × 13.5	210 × 297 mm / 8½ × 11 in
Love Hearts	8½ × 3½	9 × 20.5	420 × 297 mm / 11 × 17 in
All Tied Up	4⅜ × 8½	21 × 11	420 × 297 mm / 11 × 17 in
Driving Test	4⅜ × 8½	21 × 11	420 × 297 mm / 11 × 17 in
Easter Chick	4⅜ × 8½	21 × 11	420 × 297 mm / 11 × 17 in
Christmas Baubles	4⅜ × 8½	21 × 11	420 × 297 mm / 11 × 17 in
Shower of Gifts	6 × 8	15 × 20	420 × 297 mm / 11 × 17 in
Great News	6 × 8	15 × 20	420 × 297 mm / 11 × 17 in
Oh Christmas Tree!	5¼ × 5¼	13.5 × 13.5	210 × 297 mm / 8½ × 11 in
Birthday Surprise	4⅜ × 8½	21 × 11	420 × 297 mm / 11 × 17 in
Baby Wash Day	5⅞ × 8½	4.5 × 21	420 × 297 mm / 11 × 17 in
Graduation Day		Adapt template on page 110	
Wedding Bows		Use template on page 110	
Birthday Butterflies	4⅜ × 5¾	10 × 15	210 × 297 mm / 8½ × 11 in
Time to Sow	5⅞ × 8½	14.5 × 21	420 × 297 mm / 11 × 17 in

1 Place the completed card in the middle of a piece of paper. Fold the paper over so that it covers the card with a bit to spare and crease. Open out the paper.

2 Remove the card leaving the paper folded and fold the opposite, shorter side of paper down over the first fold and crease. Open out the paper.

3 With the card back on top of the middle section, fold in the long right side and crease the fold, followed by the left side and crease the fold.

4 Remove the card and rub over each crease with a bone folder. The dimensions of the card and envelope should now be clearly visible.

Tips
• Cut out a piece of matching paper and glue to the inside of the envelope to create a lining.

• Glue stickers, bows or buttons over the sealed end of the envelope flap.

• For bulkier cards try making a box envelope, so that the card does not get squashed. I have provided a template for a box envelope for the Wedding Bows card on page 110. You can adapt this template for other sizes and dimensions.

5 Cut away the side flaps from the top and bottom sections with a craft knife. Draw pencil lines on the shorter section to define the envelope flap. Cut away the excess and cut a curved edge around the end of the flap.

6 Apply glue to the side sections and fold up the bottom section and press down to create the envelope pocket. When ready to send, insert the card and apply a little glue along the edge and seal.

▶ Envelope templates

There is now a growing number of envelope-making kits on the market that are easy to use and that create standard-sized envelopes in no time at all. Templates are another time-saving and simple tool for making envelopes. Templates can be copied and enlarged using a personal computer, photocopier or scanner, but if you don't have these, don't worry, a sheet of tracing paper will do, using the method described below:

1. Using a sheet of tracing paper and a soft pencil draw around the template and over any fold lines marked on it.
2. Place the tracing paper with the pencilled side down on top of the paper you have chosen to make your envelope with.
4. Trace over all the pencil lines again carefully – this will transfer the pencil marks onto the envelope paper.
5. Cut out around the outer edge of the template shape with a craft knife.
6. Score and fold along the marked lines and glue where necessary to complete the envelope.

How to enlarge a template
1. Using a large sheet of acetate and a permanent black marker, draw a 1 in or 1 cm grid – depending on the units of measurement in which the original template has been made – all over the surface.
2. Place the grid over the template to assess how many squares it covers. If you want to increase the template by 100% (i.e. double it in size) and the template covers four squares – it needs to be enlarged to cover eight squares.
3. Begin to count out and draw the enlarged template shape square-by-square on the acetate.
4. Cut the new enlarged acetate template out and it is ready to use. Alternatively you could trace around this on to thick card to create a template made of card.

Tips
• Create permanent templates using heavy cardstock so that they will last.

• Make up a template for each of the project sizes and use on future projects.

Tools and Materials

If you have some experience in card making and papercrafting you may well already be equipped with much of what you need to make the projects in this book. If you are new to this craft, however, you will enjoy finding and selecting the basic items to get you started. If you are anything like me, an almost compulsive craft shopper, you will go craft shopping whether you strictly need to or not – you never know what bargains and treasures you might come across as new and wonderful materials are constantly being introduced.

Paper and card

So much variety and so much choice! Paper and card come in a vast array of shades, patterns, colours, textures and finishes. The items used in this book use primary, pastel, and metallic shades with a few patterned papers that all good craft and art outlets will stock.

Card and paper also come in a variety of weights. This is important when selecting card to be used as the base card and for making pop-up tabs and supports. Thickness and weight of card and paper are usually given in the following terms:

gsm – describes the overall weight and is short for grams per square metre.

mic – describes the overall thickness and is short for microns (1,000 microns = 1mm)

Card between 220–280 gsm is suitable as a base card as it is sturdy, easy to cut and fold and exudes quality.

Card between 100–120 gsm can be used as a base card where an outer and inner card is required, as the double thickness means the finished card will be firm enough.

Card that is over 300 gsm will be harder to cut and folds.

The thickness of card and paper can

be assessed through handling – by bending it slightly you can assess how well it will fold. When making "add-ons" – as in Baby Wash Day and Time to Sow –a thick paper, such as sugar paper, will be suitable, as it will allow for movement more easily than card.

Embossed and textured cards and papers will be thicker than they seem and are also good for "add-ons" and base cards – choose an embossed card for the outer base card and a thinner white card for the inner card.

I like to keep a range of plain papers and card of various thicknesses and weight in a stock of basic colours. A selection of mulberry paper, glitter

paper and shiny card – especially gold and silver – and pearl card and paper are also part of my basic stock.

Tips

• Keep papers and card flat to avoid creasing and damaging them. I use inexpensive desk trays and keep them on a shelf away from unwanted hands! If you are buying larger sheets of paper, perhaps gift-wrap, keep it in loose rolls, standing up in a clean bucket or basket.

Tips
• Practice with a craft knife
on scrap card– always hold
the knife straight and use a
cutting mat to protect the
surface underneath. When
cutting, turn the card
around the knife rather than
re-positioning the blade –
this creates neater cuts.

• Keep craft knives in a
sturdy plastic or metal
container for extra safety
and always replace the
safety cap between use.

Cutting, marking and scoring equipment

Long and short blade scissors

Craft knife

Metal ruler

Sturdy plastic ruler

Self-healing cutting mat

Paper trimmer

Bone folder

Embossing (scoring) tool

Soft eraser

Range of pencils 4B to 4H – "B" being soft lead, "H" being hard lead

Tweezers and toothpicks for picking up and fixing embellishments

Fine and thick black, silver and gold marker pens

Fibre tip pens for adding small amounts of colour and outlining.

Adhesives

All of the following are essential adhesives and have been used in the projects in this book.

Glue sticks come in various sizes and are so easy to use. The strength of glue from a stick is surprisingly good.

"Tacky" glue is a bit stronger, clear drying and ideal for gluing bows, buttons and other embellishments.

Glitter glue is great for adding sparkle and can be found in a wide range of colours.

General craft glue is an economical and clear drying alternative to a glue stick.

Double-sided sticky tape comes in a range of thicknesses. Best used where there is minimal need for accuracy in positioning – once applied it is difficult to remove!

Sticky pads can be purchased in various sizes or on rolls and contribute to the 3D effect of embellishments.

Clear sticky tape is ideal for use where the tape will not be seen.

Masking tape is great for temporary positioning.

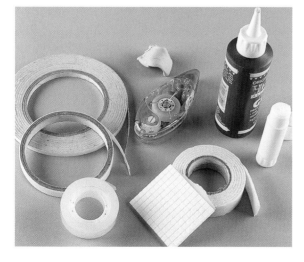

Tips
• When using wet glues
remember to wash your
hands regularly to avoid
leaving unsightly glue marks.

• Use toothpicks (cocktail
sticks) for applying small
amounts of glue

• Stick masking tape to your
clothing before use to make
the tape even less tacky and
easier to remove.

Tips
• To care for your punches, punch into tin foil or wax paper and keep away from moisture when not in use.

• When punching shapes, keep the discarded outline as a possible embellishment for future projects.

Paper punches

Punches come in different styles allowing you to cut whole images, geometric shapes, fancy borders or snip corners. Stock up on basic punches, such as different-sized circles, squares, flowers, hearts and stars that will be flexible enough to use on a wide variety of themes and occasions.

Tips
• Heat tools get very hot very quickly and need to be handled with care.

• Use tweezers to hold small items when heating them to avoid burning fingers.

• Wipe the area to be embossed with an anti-static bag – this helps to stop embossing powder sticking on areas where you don't want it.

• You can make your own anti-static bag. Cut a circle of wash cloth, fill with talc and sew the edges together. Add a second layer of cloth and sew again.

Embossing tools

Embossing ink pads are designed to stay "wet" so that the image can be covered in embossing powder. **Embossing powder** is fine powder that can be found in a wide range of colours and finishes and is applied over embossing ink.

Heat tools quickly heat to the required temperature to set embossing powders and pigment ink.

Rubber stamps and ink pads

A small selection of stamps have been used in some of the designs in this book (see New Home and Time to Sow). They are great for giving you an image that can then be coloured, embossed or decorated in a variety of ways. Stamps can also easily be found to co-ordinate with other parts of the overall design. A range of inkpads is essential when using stamps. They come in all sorts of colours and are usually either water based or pigment based.

Water-based ink is fast drying so does not need time to dry.

Pigment ink takes time to dry but is more useful for embossing and using on shiny surfaces – such as metallic card – where water-based ink would smear.

Tips

- Always clean stamps properly and allow them to dry before putting away.

- Store stamps out of direct sunlight and rubber side down.

Tips

- Recycle bits and pieces from around the house to build up a collection of embellishments.

- Keep cards that you have received; there may be parts of them you can use on future projects.

Embellishments

This term refers to all those small items that can be used to decorate a card: buttons, ribbons, bows, beads, wire, peel-offs and brads are just a small example. Because pop-up cards can be bulky, consider the thickness of embellishments and remember – the bulkier the finished card – the larger the envelope it will need.

baby carriage

difficulty
level ◆

A simple yet effective card using
pastel shades to offer a warm welcome to any new arrival – and to
pass on your congratulations to the proud parents. The message box
inside the card provides a neat space for a personalized greeting. The design
of this card can be adapted to suit a boy or girl by selecting shades of
either pink or blue.

You will need

Paper/Card

- ▶ 210 x 148 mm (8¼ x 5¾ in) white card
- ▶ 210 x 148 mm (8¼ x 5¾ in) lemon card
- ▶ 210 x 148 mm (8¼ x 5¾ in) paper in peach, sage, lilac and lemon
- ▶ Scrap white card
- ▶ Scrap pale blue paper

Equipment

- ▶ Pencil
- ▶ Embossing tool
- ▶ Bone folder
- ▶ Eraser
- ▶ Scissors
- ▶ 2½ cm (1¼ in) circle punch
- ▶ 1 cm (½ in) circle punch
- ▶ ½ cm (¼ in) circle punch
- ▶ Tiny cross punch
- ▶ Decorative border punch
- ▶ Glue stick
- ▶ Double-sided sticky tape
- ▶ Lilac ink pad
- ▶ 15 cm (6 in) thin lilac ribbon
- ▶ Yellow, pale blue, lilac and pink assorted buttons

Tips

- • Arrange the punched crosses and circles on the inside before gluing in place.

- • Replace the crosses along the bottom front of the card with a greeting.

▶ Inside of card

1 Mark a pencil line across the centre of the 210 x 148 mm (8¼ x 5¾ in) white card. Score the line with the embossing tool, fold in half and rub a bone folder across the fold.

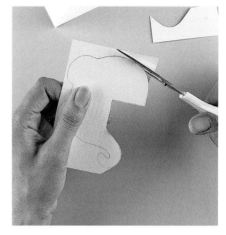

2 Using the template on page 92, draw and cut out the inside pram from yellow card. Erase all pencil marks.

3 Using the ½ cm (¼ in) circle punch, punch two circles from peach paper, three from blue paper, two from sage paper and two from lilac paper. Using the 2½ cm/1¼ in) punch, punch two circles from peach paper. Using the cross punch, punch two lemon crosses. Using the glue stick, glue the large peach circles over the yellow pram wheels. Glue a cross in the middle of each wheel. Glue the tiny circles over the surface of the pram.

4 Punch out the border using the border punch from lilac paper. Against the punched edge, draw a circular bonnet shape – so the punched edge becomes the bonnet frill. Punch a 2½ cm (1¼ in) circle from peach paper. Draw and cut a fat heart shape on this circle. Tie a small bow in the thin ribbon and trim the ends.

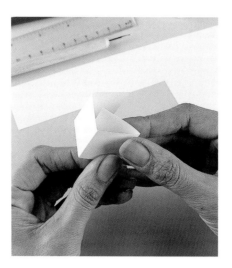

5 Cut out the bonnet and face and glue together. Glue the face behind the pram hood. Glue the bow in front. Add a small pencil line to highlight the baby's eye.

6 Cut a length of white card 3.5 × 12 cm (1⅜ × 4¾ in). Mark a pencil line every 3 cm (1⅛ in) until you have four sections. Groove along the lines using the embossing tool. Erase pencil marks. Fold along the grooves to form a rectangle.

7 Secure the end sections of the rectangle with sticky tape. Position the rectangle right into the centre fold in the middle of the base card. Fix in place with double-sided sticky tape or glue.

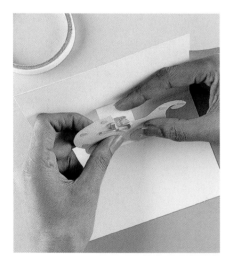

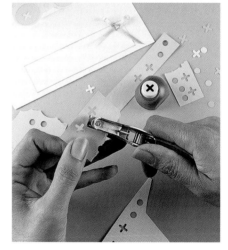

8 Fix a piece of double-sided sticky tape to the front section of the white rectangle. Peel off the backing and fix the pram in place – allowing it to sit slightly higher than the bottom of the rectangle.

9 Cut a rectangle of white card 10.5 × 3 cm (4⅛ × 1⅛ in). Rub the edges of the rectangle in the lilac ink pad. Fix the rectangle to the bottom inside edge of the card using double-sided sticky tape. Make another small bow out of the thin ribbon and trim the ends. Glue the bow to the top right corner of this rectangle.

10 Punch a selection of tiny circles and crosses from the coloured papers. Glue randomly over the inside areas of the card to complete.

▶ Front of card

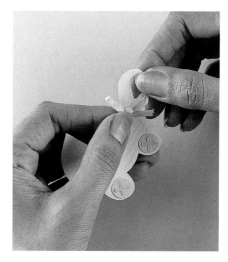

11 Cut a strip of lemon paper 2 cm (¾ in) in depth and long enough to fit across the long edge of the card. Cut a second long strip from peach paper. Cut two shorter strips, also 2 cm (¾ in) in depth, long enough to fit the short sides of the card from lilac and sage paper.

12 Leave a narrow white border when gluing each strip. Glue the sage strip down the right side of the card. Glue the lilac strip down the opposite side. Glue the peach strip along the bottom. Glue the lemon strip across the top. Trim any excess.

13 Using the template on page 92, draw and cut out a small pram from lemon card. Punch two 1 cm (½ in) circles from peach paper. Punch two crosses from lilac paper. Glue the circles onto the wheels, and the crosses onto the circles. Tie a small bow and glue onto the handle. Glue the pram in the centre of the card.

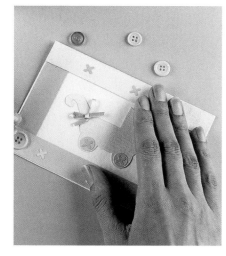

14 Punch six crosses from the coloured papers. Glue three across the top lemon strip. Glue three across the bottom peach strip. Glue the buttons at the corners to complete the front design.

funny frog

difficulty level ◆

This cheeky chap will certainly bring a smile to a child's face on his or her birthday, and is bound to brighten the day of anyone who needs cheering up. The colour scheme can be adapted to shades of silver, turquoise and pink, to give a more contemporary and adult feel. Change the frog to a pumpkin to create a Halloween card.

You will need

Paper/Card

▸ 210 x 297 mm (8½ x 11 in) white card
▸ 210 x 297 mm (8½ x 11 in) pale green card
▸ 210 x 297 mm (8½ x 11 in) in two further shades of green paper
▸ Paper scraps – brown, black, white, yellow, red

Equipment

▸ Pencil
▸ Ruler
▸ Eraser
▸ Scissors
▸ Craft knife
▸ Cutting mat
▸ 2.5 cm (1¼ in) circle punch
▸ 1 cm (½ in) circle punch
▸ Glue stick
▸ Small sticky pads
▸ Double-sided sticky tape

Tip
Write your message over the grass on the inside of the card.

Inside of card

1 Using the template on page 93, draw a frog on pale green card, and mark all the pencil lines as shown. Cut out the frog shape. Using the craft knife and a cutting mat, cut along the horizontal line.

2 Fold the frog in half – so the markings are visible. Fold the middle sections to the right and left of the cut, up and back – along the visible pencil lines.

3 Return the sections to their original position and open out the template. Rub away all pencil lines. Tease the central cuts forward at the same time as folding the frog inward – the "mouth" should now open out as the frog is closed.

4 Using the eye template on page 94 draw and cut two eyes from white scrap paper. Punch two large circles from black paper using the 2.5cm (1¼ in) punch, and two small circles using the 1 cm (½ in) punch from white paper. Glue the small white circles onto the large black circles and glue onto the eye shape.

5 Cut four strips of white paper 1 cm × 10 cm (¼ × 4 in). Glue one strip to the end of another at right angles. Begin to fold each strip over the other – creating a concertina spring. Glue the ends together. Repeat the process with the other two strips. Fix a spring to the back of each eye, and stick the springy eyes to the frog with sticky pads.

6 Using the circle punches, punch six large circles and seven small circles from scrap yellow paper, and glue onto the frog. Using the template on page 94, draw and cut out the frog's tongue from scrap red paper and glue to the inside of the upper right lip of the mouth.

7 Cut a piece of white card 29 × 21 cm (11½ × 8¼ inch). Fold in half to create the base card. Cut out two grass pieces using the templates on page 94. Draw and cut four bulrushes from scrap brown paper, and thin stems from green paper. Cut a square of red paper 8 × 8 cm (3¼ × 3¼ in). Draw and cut two further pieces of grass from dark green paper – slightly smaller than the first.

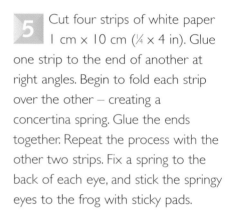

8 Open out the base card and glue the lighter grass pieces to the right and left of the opened card – leaving the short front stems free of glue. Glue the red paper square 4 cm (1⅝ in) down from the top of the card – ensuring it sits centrally across the fold.

9 Apply double-sided sticky tape to the back of the frog. Stick the frog 2.5 cm (1¼ in) down from the top of the centre fold. Ensure that the card folds flat and the frog sits in the middle. Tuck him behind those free blades of grass. Apply glue to the front stems of grass and glue over the frog's feet.

10 Glue the darker green grasses over the top. Glue the paper stems onto the bulrushes and glue onto the card, making sure that the edges of the stems are flush neatly with the edges of the blades of grass. (If you tuck the stems behind the grass, this will leave ridges that show through the green paper grass.)

Front of card

11 Using the templates on page 94 draw and cut the top of the frog from pale green card. Make two eyes as you did in step 4, but without the small white circles on top. Draw and cut the grass from dark green paper. Draw and cut a second grass piece smaller than the first. Make up three bulrushes as in step 7.

12 Glue the two layers of grass together, then stick to the front of the card, leaving the top parts unglued. Tuck the frog behind, then glue down the blades of grass.

Tip
To give depth to the front design, fix the bulrushes using small sticky pads.

new home

difficulty
level ◆

Receiving the keys and opening the door to step over the threshold of a new home is a very exciting moment. The task of unpacking the boxes and deciding where things go awaits! The front of this card is kept simple enabling a message to be written across the top, or even on the little label in the letterbox. You could also add the number of the new house to the front door.

You will need

Paper/Card

- ▶ Two 210 x 297 mm (8½ x 11 in) sheets of white card
- ▶ 210 x 148 mm (8¼ x 5¾ in) selection of textured brown and cream papers
- ▶ Scrap green print paper
- ▶ Scrap, peach and dark brown paper

Equipment

- ▶ Pencil
- ▶ Ruler
- ▶ Embossing tool
- ▶ Bone folder
- ▶ Paper trimmer
- ▶ Eraser
- ▶ Scissors
- ▶ Glue stick
- ▶ Key rubber stamp
- ▶ Cocoa-colour ink pad
- ▶ Craft knife
- ▶ Cutting mat
- ▶ Thin natural-coloured string
- ▶ Thick natural-coloured string
- ▶ Tiny fern punch
- ▶ Tiny pot punch
- ▶ Medium gift-tag punch
- ▶ Tiny gift-tag punch
- ▶ Red marker pen
- ▶ 2.5 cm (1¼ in) circle punch
- ▶ 1 cm (½ in) circle punch
- ▶ Glitter glue
- ▶ Tiny gold brad
- ▶ Sticky pads
- ▶ Patterned-edge scissors

▶ Inside of card

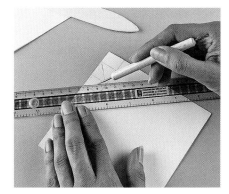

1 Cut, score and fold two pieces of white card 27 x 13.5 cm (10⅝ x 5¼ in). On the outside front of one card draw three 2 cm (¾ in) long horizontal lines 1.5 cm (⅝ in), 3.5 cm (1⅜ in) and 5 cm (2 in) down the right hand side of the centre fold. Draw a vertical line down the right side to create three sections. Draw a diagonal line from the top left to the bottom right of the middle section.

2 Fold the card in half and cut along the diagonal line with scissors. Using the embossing tool, groove a line from the inner end of the cut to the bottom left-hand corner of the bottom section.

3 Rub away all pencil lines. Open the card and gently tease forward the cut section. Close the card and rub with the bone folder to give a neat crease. Open again – the pop up should now be completed.

4 Cut two paper rectangles (brown and cream) 5 x 2.5 cm (2 x 1 in). Cut a cream textured paper rectangle 4.5 x 6 cm (1¾ x 2⅜ in). Cut a cream-paper round-ended rectangle 3 x 4 cm (1⅛ x 1⅝ in). Punch two tiny tags from cream paper. Cut a thin brown paper strip roughly 5 cm (2 in) long. Cut three paper squares (two cream, one peach) 4.5 x 4.5 cm (1¾ x 1¾ in).

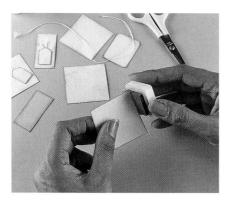

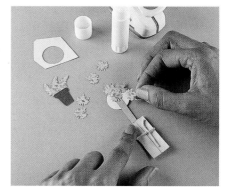

5 Ink the edges of all the "crates" and tags. Cut two pieces of thin string and glue onto one cream square in a cross pattern, as if it is tied around the crate. Cut tiny pieces of thin string and glue to the tops of each tag. Glue one tag horizontally across the cream rectangle. Glue the second tag at an angle on the bottom left of the larger rectangle.

6 Punch three fern leaves from green printed paper. Punch a tiny flowerpot from dark brown paper. Punch eight maple leaves from green printed paper. Cut out a square of cream paper 4.5 × 4.5 cm (1¾ × 1¾ in) and ink the edges.

7 Glue the fern leaves to the top of the flower pot. Glue one end of the strip of brown paper (the tree trunk) to the peach paper square. Fold in the sides of the square over the tree trunk so an inked edge sits in front, and glue. Tie a piece of thin string around this in a knot. Punch a 2.5 cm (1¼ in) circle from scrap white card and glue behind the top end of the tree trunk. Arrange and glue the maple leaves to the white circle.

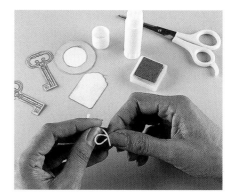

8 Glue the outer card (left over from step 1) to the inner card (the one with the pop-up element), with the pop up at the top. Glue all the items in place as shown above and in the main picture on page 24. Cut out a few small squares of cream paper and draw 'This Way Up' arrows on them with red marker pen. Stick these onto the crates.

9 Ink the key stamp with black ink and stamp two keys onto brown paper. Using the template on page 95 draw and cut out the key ring from brown card. Cut out the inner circle with a craft knife, leaning on the cutting mat. Draw and cut a second key ring from white paper, but leave the middle circle intact. Punch a medium tag from cream paper.

10 Drag the edges of the keys, brown key ring and tag with the cocoa ink pad. Glue the white ring behind the brown ring. Cut a length of thick string and tie into a bow.

11 Position and glue the key ring to the left side of the pop-up – check that the card closes neatly while the glue is still tacky, in case you need to reposition. Glue the keys to the top of the ring – again check that the card closes neatly. Bend the top section of the tag to fit over part of the ring and glue in place. Glue the string bow in place at the top of the gift tag. Leave to dry.

▶ Front of card

12 Using the templates on page 95, cut out the two rectangles and two door covers from brown paper. Ink the edges with the ink pad. Cut a patterned-edge strip of brown paper, longer than the door cover. Glue this strip behind one of the door covers, so the edge still shows. Cut two 0.5 cm (¼ in) wide strips of brown paper, the length of the larger rectangle, and ink the edges. Glue the small rectangle onto the larger one.

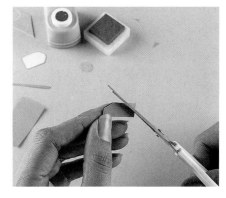

13 Punch a 1 cm (½ in) circle from brown paper. Punch a tiny tag from cream paper – ink the edges. Cut a small square from the same shade of brown paper. Fold the square in half and trim off the corners to create a letter box.

14 Punch two 2.5 cm (1¼ in) circles from green printed paper to create tree foliage. Cut two strips of brown paper for the trunks. Punch two small pots from dark brown paper. Add small dots of glitter glue to each foliage circle and let dry. Assemble and glue the pots, trunks and foliage circles to create two small trees.

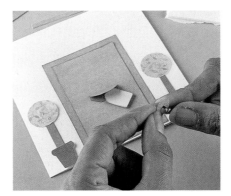

15 Glue the rectangular door in the middle of the card front. Glue the letter box onto the door – the top section should open forward. Punch a 1 cm (½ in) circle of brown paper. Push the gold brad though it and fix above the letter box with a sticky pad. Glue the tag just under the letter-box flap. Glue the two potted trees either side of the door.

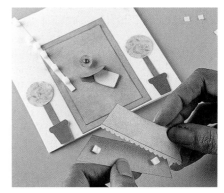

16 Fix the two thin strips from step 12 using sticky pads on top of the side strips on the front door. Fix the door cover over the first – using sticky pads. Stick the two side strips and the door cover on the door to create the 3D effect.

thinking of you

difficulty
level ◆   A versatile card letting someone know
that you care, whether the occasion be a
birthday, get-well or a special thank you. There is space
on the front and inside for you to personalize it with
your own greeting and message.

You will need

Paper/Card

▸ 210 x 297 mm (8½ x 11 in) white paper

▸ 210 x 297 mm (8½ x 11 in) white card

▸ 210 x 148 mm (8¼ x 5¾ in) lemon card

▸ 210 x 148 mm (8¼ x 5¾ in) yellow-spot paper

▸ Scrap lime paper

Equipment

▸ Pencil

▸ Ruler

▸ Bone folder

▸ Paper trimmer

▸ Eraser

▸ Daisy 'background' rubber stamp

▸ Lime ink pad

▸ 1 cm (½ in) circle punch

▸ Glue stick

▸ Scissors

▸ Yellow fibre marker

▸ Clear sticky tape

▸ ½ cm (¼ inch) circle punch

▸ Medium daisy punch

▸ Small sticky pads

▸ Inside of card

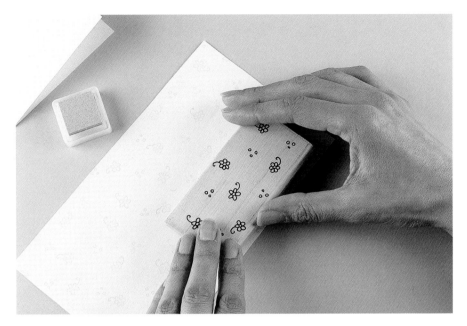

1 Fold in half the 210 x 148 mm (8¼ x 5¾ in) piece of lemon card and rub the fold with the bone folder. Ink the background daisy stamp with lime ink and stamp onto a piece of white paper roughly 20 x 4.5 cm (8 x 2 in). Continue stamping until the paper is covered.

2 Measure, mark and cut three strips 15 x 1.5 cm (5⅞ x ⅝ in) from the yellow-spot paper. Punch four circles from lime paper using the 1 cm (½ in) circle punch. Measure, mark and cut three strips 20 x 1.5 cm (7⅞ x ⅝ in) from the stamped paper. Leave a strip of each paper to one side.

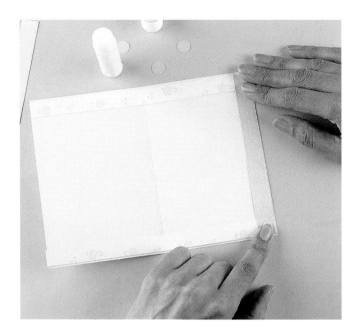

3 Glue the stamped strips across the top and bottom of the card again leaving a slim lemon border showing. Glue the yellow-spot strips to the right and left sides of the lemon card – leaving a slim lemon border showing. Trim away any excess. Glue the four lime-coloured circles to the corners of the card.

4 Using the template on page 95, draw and cut out four daisies in white card. Remember, move the card around the scissors, not the scissors around the card, in order to get neater edges. Fold the daisies in half and open out. Rub away all pencil marks. Use the yellow marker pen to colour the tops of each daisy.

5 Glue the left side of one daisy to the right side of another. Glue the left side of this daisy to the right side of a third daisy. Glue the left side of this daisy to the right side of the last daisy. Glue the left side of this daisy to the right side of the first daisy. Leave to dry.

6 Cut a thin piece of lime paper into a curved shape for the stalk, and glue to the back of the daisy. Apply glue to the back of daisy and stalk. Position the daisy 3.5 cm (1½ in) down from the top of the card and across the centre fold – press down the daisy and the stalk firmly.

▶ Front of card

7 Punch three ½ cm (¼ in) circles from lime paper. Punch six ½ cm (¼ in) circles from yellow-spot paper. Punch three daisies from white paper. Cut three ½ × 6 cm (¼ × 2⅜ in) strips of lime paper.

8 Glue the remaining stamped strip across the top and the remaining yellow-spot strip across the bottom of the card, leaving slim borders of lemon card showing, and trim. Glue three yellow circles across the stamped strip and three lime circles across the yellow-spot strip. Glue the lime stems vertically in the centre of the card. Glue three yellow circles onto the daisies. Fix the daisies onto the stems using sticky pads.

Tips
• If the strips of stamped paper do not hold many flower images, you can add a few more using just the corner flower of the stamp.

• Don't worry about the edges of the pop-up daisy not aligning perfectly once glued together – this simply adds to the realism of the petals.

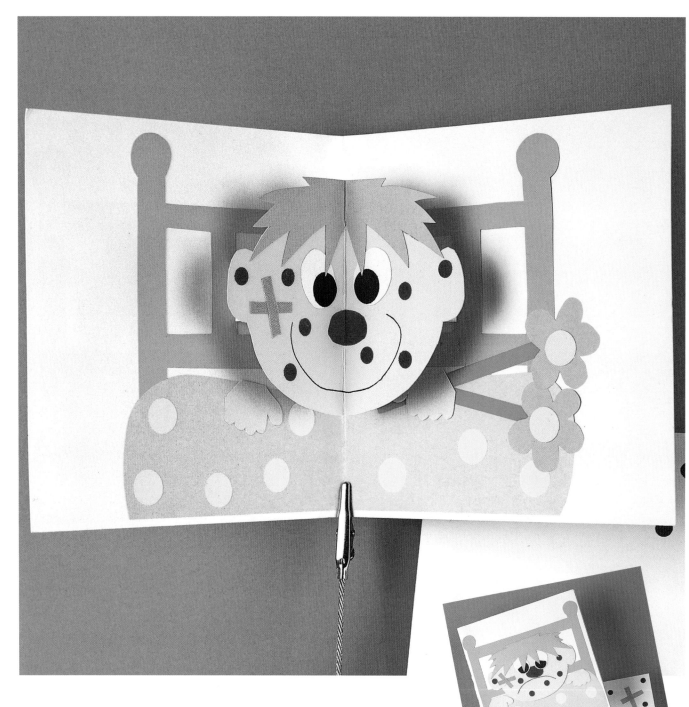

get well soon

difficulty level ◆◆

Here's something bright and cheerful to raise the spirits of anyone who is ill. The contrast between the miserable face on the front and the happy face inside reflects the difference this card will make. You can make a matching envelope by repeating the dressing strip and spots from the card.

You will need

Paper/Card

▶ 210 x 297 mm (8½ x 11 in)
white card

▶ 210 x 148 mm (8¼ x 5¾ in) papers
in pale blue, peach, sand and
light green

▶ Paper scraps in red, black, white,
yellow and pink

Equipment

▶ Pencil

▶ Ruler

▶ Paper trimmer

▶ Eraser

▶ Embossing tool

▶ Scissors

▶ Glue stick

▶ ½ cm (¼ in) circle punch

▶ 1 cm (½ in) circle punch

▶ Roll or strips of plaster/band aid

▶ Black marker pen

▶ Inside of card

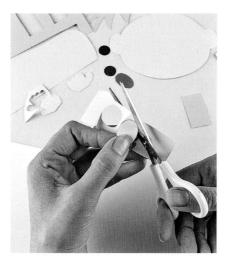

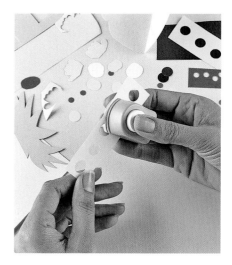

1 Measure and cut a piece of white card 28 x 14 cm (11 x 5½ in). Fold in half, open out and rub away all pencil marks. Using the templates on pages 96–7 draw and cut out the large bed from pale blue paper; large blanket from green paper; large head and hands from peach; small hair from sand paper; and two eye pieces from white. Draw and cut a small nose from red paper.

2 Punch eight ½ cm (¼ in) circles from red paper. Punch eight 1 cm (½ in) circles from yellow paper. Punch two 1 cm (½ in) circles from black paper.

3 Glue the black circles to the white eyes and glue onto the face. Glue on the nose, spots and hair – allowing the hair to cover part of the eyes. Use the embossing tool to score a vertical line down the middle of the face, and fold inwards gently. Cut two tiny strips of plaster/band aid and stick to the left side of the face in a cross. Using the black marker draw in a happy smile.

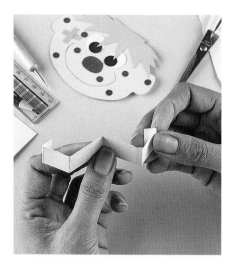

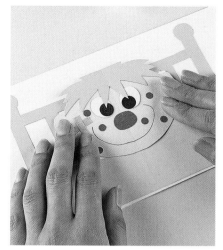

4 Draw and cut out a 2 × 12 cm (¾ × 4¾ in) strip of white card and fold it in half. Fold each half in half again, backwards from the central fold. Fold back two shorter tabs on each end.

5 Glue the bed across the centre of the card and the blanket across the bottom. Glue the folded support strip across the back of the completed face.

6 Apply glue to the tab ends of the support strip. Position and glue the strip and face so it sits flat across the middle of the card in front of the bed frame and blanket. As the card closes, the face will move forward.

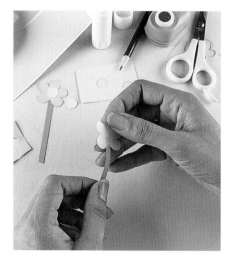

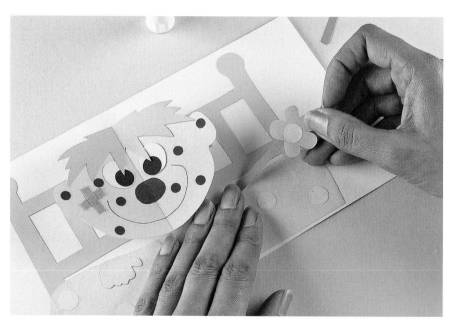

7 Using the template on page 97 cut two flower heads from pink paper. Punch two 1 cm (½ in) circles from peach paper. Cut two thin strips from green paper. Glue these pieces together to make up the flowers.

8 Punch some 1 cm (½ in) yellow circles and glue them over the blanket. Glue the flowers to the right side of the card. Glue

the hands in place – ensuring the right-side hand goes over the flower stems.

Front of card

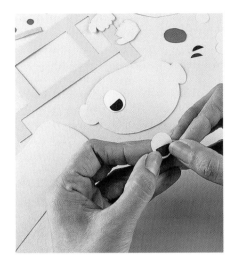

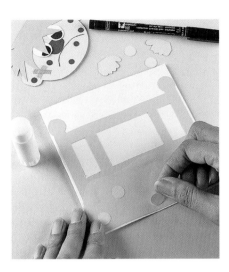

10 Position and glue the bed and blanket to the card. Make up the face as you did in step 3. Cut part of the black circles away and glue onto the white eye pieces. Draw a black marker line for the sad mouth, then glue the face on top of the bed. Glue yellow circles to the blanket and glue the hands in place to finish off.

9 Using the templates on pages 96–7 draw and cut the out the small bed frame, small blanket, small face, hands and the large hair, all in the same colours as before. Punch six ½ cm (¼ in) red circles. Punch five yellow and two black 1 cm (½ in) circles. Draw and cut two white eye pieces, and a larger red nose. Cut two strips of plaster/band aid.

Tips
• Cut out all the pieces for both the front and the inside together to save time.

• Add a small tag to the flowers for adding the recipient's name.

• The design can be adapted to show a female face by adding longer hair and eyelashes.

• Use the colours of the recipient's bedroom to make it even more personalized.

love hearts

difficulty
level ◆

Perfect for Valentine's Day or as a birthday card to that special person, this elegant design allows you plenty of room to write or stamp your own romantic message inside the card.

You will need

Paper/Card

▸ Two 210 x 297 mm (8½ x 11 in) white cards

▸ 210 x 297 mm (8½ x 11 in) red card

▸ Scrap gold, holographic gold and white mulberry papers

Equipment

▸ Pencil

▸ Ruler

▸ Paper trimmer

▸ Embossing tool

▸ Bone folder

▸ Eraser

▸ Double-sided sticky tape

▸ Scissors

▸ Clear embossing ink pad

▸ Embossing pen

▸ Gold embossing powder

▸ Heat tool

▸ Small heart punch

▸ Glue stick

▸ 10 cm (3⅞ in) wide loose-weave gold ribbon

▸ Gold star brad

▶ Inside of card

1 Measure and cut a piece of white card 18 x 20.5 cm (7⅛ x 8 in) – the outer card. Measure and cut a second piece 17 x 19.5 cm (6⅝ x 7⅝) – the inner card. Mark a pencil line lengthwise down the centre of each piece. Score with the embossing tool and fold using the bone folder. Rub away pencil marks.

2 Lay the inner card horizontally in front of you with the fold at the top. Draw a pencil line 4.5 cm (1¾ in) in from the left side, and another 5.5 cm (2⅛ in) in from the right side.

3 Fold the top right corner inward so the folded edge sits along the pencil line. Rub the fold with the bone folder to give a neat crease. Repeat on the left side.

4 Open out the card and rub away all pencil lines. Tease the folds forward and fold the card again. Rub with the bone folder and open out. Fix double-sided sticky tape to the back and fix onto the outer card.

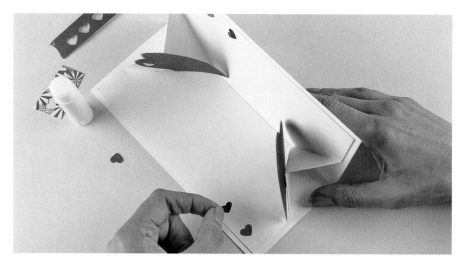

5 Using the template on page 98, draw and cut two large hearts from red card. Run the edges across the clear embossing ink pad. Apply gold embossing powder and heat with a heat tool.

6 Punch two small hearts from gold holographic paper. Punch six hearts from gold paper. Glue the holographic hearts to the corners of the red hearts. Apply glue to the inner left-hand sides of the pop-out sections on the card. Position a heart against the glue and secure in place. Glue three tiny gold hearts down the top right edge of the card. Glue three tiny gold hearts down the bottom left edge of the card.

▶ Front of card

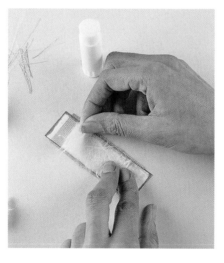

7 Cut a piece of white card 10.5 x 3 cm (4⅛ x 1⅛ in). Emboss the edges with gold embossing powder (just like you embossed the edges of the hearts in step 5). Cut a piece of gold ribbon slightly shorter than the piece of card. Tease out the outer threads of the ribbon, and pull out strands all the way around the four edges.

8 Tear a piece of mulberry paper slightly smaller than the size of the ribbon. Glue the ribbon onto the card piece slightly off centre to the right. Glue the mulberry paper on top of the ribbon.

9 Using the template on page 98 draw and cut the slim heart from red card. Emboss the edges with gold embossing powder. Using the embossing pen, mark a cross in the heart, cover with gold embossing powder and emboss with the heat tool.

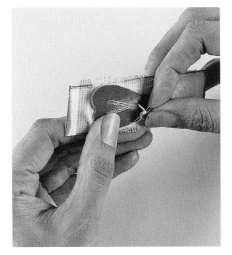

10 Use the embossing tool to pierce a small hole through the slim heart. Insert the brad and fold back the tabs. Glue the heart on top of the mulberry paper. Glue the whole piece to the front of the card.

Tips

• When fixing the hearts to the inside of the card, test their position first by using Blu-tack. Close the card to check the hearts stay within the card when closed. Only then apply the glue.

• If you do not have an embossing pen – drag the short end of a small ruler across the embossing ink pad and mark a cross.

• Store embossing powder in plastic boxes large enough to dip card into.

• When using the heat tool, keep it away from anything that might catch light.

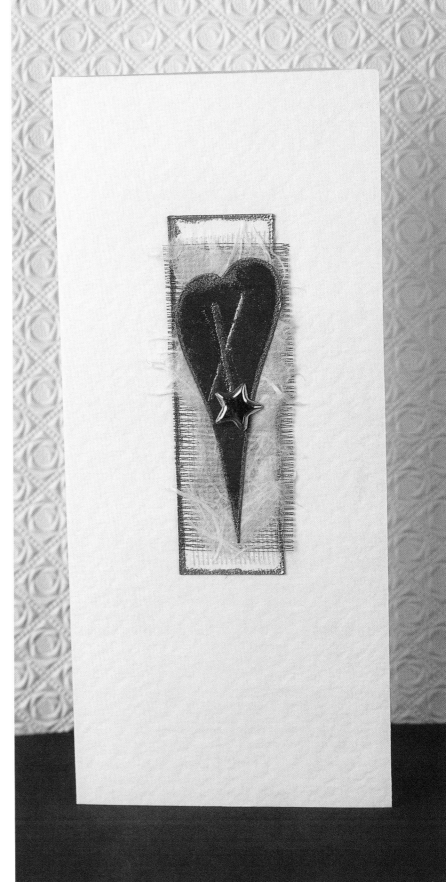

all tied up

difficulty
level ◆◆
Designing cards for men can be a
challenge so this card is versatile enough
to be used on many different occasions. It could even
be given as a Christmas card if it is accompanied by a gift of a new tie – just add
tiny Christmas-tree decorations and tinsel across the top of the wardrobe!

You will need

Paper/Card

▸ 210 x 297 mm (8½ x 11 in) white card

▸ 210 x 297 mm (8½ x 11 in) papers in pale blue, salmon, sand, striped, mottled brown and sage colours

▸ 210 x 148 mm (8¼ x 5¾ in) pale brown card

▸ White scrap card

Equipment

▸ Pencil
▸ Ruler
▸ Embossing tool
▸ Eraser
▸ Cutting mat
▸ Glue stick
▸ Black marker pen
▸ Scissors
▸ 12 cm (4¾ in) length of black wire
▸ Craft knife
▸ Double-sided sticky tape
▸ 10 tiny silver brads
▸ Small cross punch
▸ Water-based black ink pad
▸ Red marker pen

Inside of card

1 Cut a piece of white card 21 x 2 cm (8¼ x 8¼ in). Make a groove down the centre using a ruler and the embossing tool. Fold in half and run the bone folder along the fold to create a neat edge. Rub away all pencil marks. Measure and cut four strips of paper 1 x 21 cm (½ x 8¼ in) – one each of sage, salmon, pale blue and striped. Glue these around the inside edges of the white card leaving a slim white border all around.

2 Using the black marker and the tie template on page 99 draw and cut four ties – one each of sage, sand, pale blue and striped papers. Using a black marker, add dots to the sage tie and fold back all top tabs.

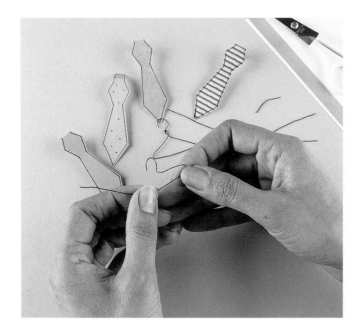

3 Cut four 12 cm (4¾ in) lengths of wire. Using the template on page 99 as a guide, bend the wire into a clothes-hanger shape and trim off any excess wire.

4 Using the black marker and the template on page 99, draw and cut the two shelf pieces from pale brown card. Pierce a hole in each of the circles using the craft knife. Fold shelf-piece 1 so the centre fold goes backward. Fold shelf-piece 2 so the centre fold and the side tabs all come forward.

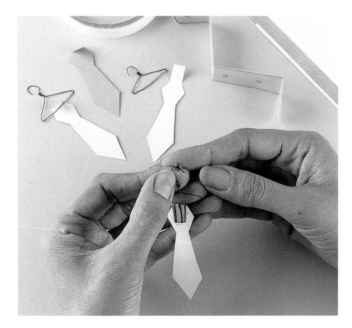

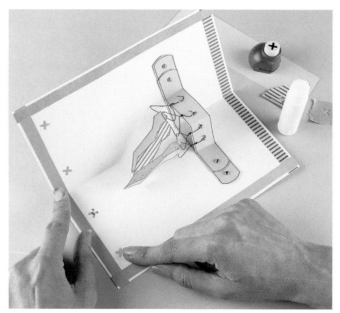

5 Using double-sided sticky tape fix each tie onto a hanger, ensuring the ties can move freely. Open the pins of eight brads and push the top of each hanger though the pins of a brad. Close the pins and fix the brads through all the holes in the shelf. When the brads are opened at the back – the ties will be firmly fixed in place.

6 Using double-sided sticky tape – fix shelf piece 2 to shelf piece 1 to create the shelf. Fix the completed shelf to the white card 5 cm (2 in) down from the top of the card and ensuring that the folds sit comfortably together. Punch a small cross from each of the papers and glue in place along the bottom of the card.

▶ Front of card

7 Using black marker and the template on page 99, cut a piece of mottled brown paper for the wardrobe. Draw a black line 3 cm (1⅛ in) in from the right and left – giving you a double line down the centre of the paper. Drag the edges of the paper along the black inkpad.

8 Make up a hanger as you did in step 3. Cut a tie from white scrap card. Cut thin strips of red paper and glue across the tie at an angle. Trim off excess. Fix a brad outside the double lines of the wardrobe and secure at the back. Fix the hanger with tie to the remaining brad and secure at the back of the wardrobe, so it now has two door knobs. Glue the wardrobe to the front of the card.

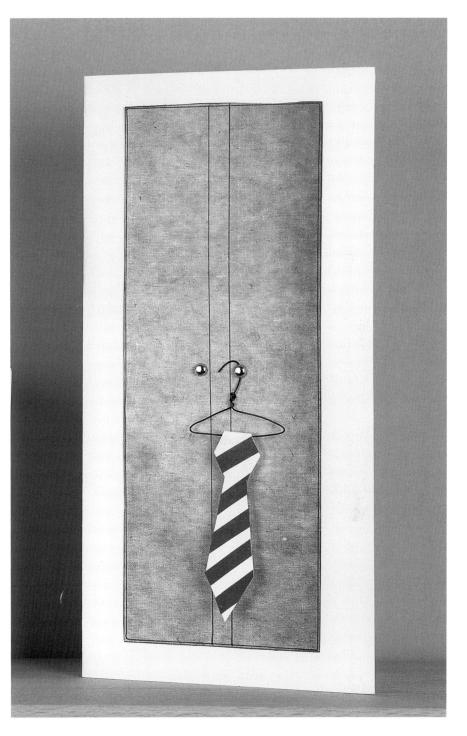

Tips
• To reduce the bulkiness of the card – replace the brads with circles of silver card.

• Try using colourful wrapping paper stuck to thin card to make the ties.

• To congratulate someone on a new job, replace the ties with clothes suitable for that profession.

• Adapt the design for a female by putting female clothes and accessories on the hangers.

driving test

difficulty
level ◆◆

A car-themed card here, ideal for anyone who has just passed their driving test, or as a birthday greeting for a someone mad about cars! You can add an appropriate message along the top or bottom of the card, either inside or on the front. The colour scheme has been created for a male recipient but could easily be changed for a female using different colours.

You will need

Paper/Card

▸ 210 x 297 mm (8½ x 11 in) black card

▸ 210 x 297 mm (8½ x 11 in) grey card

▸ 210 x 297 mm (8½ x 11 in) red shiny card

▸ 210 x 148 mm (8¼ x 5¾ in) patterned grey paper

▸ 210 x 148 mm (8¼ x 5¾ in) plain grey paper

▸ Scrap silver paper

▸ Scrap black paper

▸ Scrap white card

Equipment

▸ Pencil

▸ Ruler

▸ Eraser

▸ Paper trimmer

▸ Scissors

▸ Black marker pen

▸ Permanent black marker pen

▸ Glue stick

▸ Clear sticky tape

▸ ½ cm (¼ in) circle punch

▸ Approximately 15 cm (6 in) thin wire

▸ Sticky pads

▶ Inside of card

1 Measure and cut a piece of grey card 21 x 21 cm (8¼ x 8¼ in). Fold in half, open out and rub away all pencil marks. Measure and cut a piece of black card 20 x 14 cm (7⅞ x 5½ in). Fold in half and cut a wavy line from the outer edges. Rub away all pencil marks.

2 Take the folded black card with the folded edge nearest you. In pencil draw two 1.5 cm- (⅝ in-) long vertical lines, 2 cm (¾ in) and 4 cm (1⅝ in) in from the left edge. Join the tops of these two lines with a horizontal line. Draw two 3 cm- (1⅛ in-) long vertical lines, 7.5 cm (3 in) and 12.5 cm (4⅞ in) in from the left side and join these with a horizontal line. Draw two 1.5 cm- (⅝ in-) long vertical lines, 16 cm (6¼ in) and 18 cm (7⅛ in) in from the left side and join these with a horizontal line. Cut along all the vertical lines.

3 Fold the cut sections towards you, straighten, fold away from you and straighten again. Open the card and push the cut sections forward.

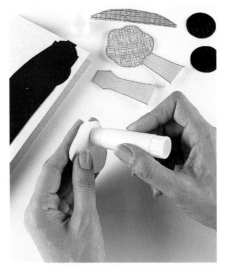

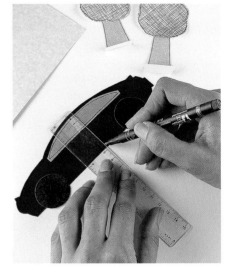

4 Use the templates on page 98. In black pen draw then cut out two tree tops from patterned grey paper. In permanent black pen draw then cut out the car from shiny red card. Cut out the window from silver paper; two wheels from black paper; two tree trunks from plain grey card.

5 Fold the bottom of the tree trunks forward to create a stand. Glue the tree tops to the trunks leaving no more than 1.5 cm (⅝ in) between the top of the trunk and the top of the tree when glued – this will ensure the trees remain inside the card when completed.

6 Glue the wheels and window to the car. Using the permanent marker draw a line across the bottom of the car. Draw a second line through the window and down to the bottom line. Draw in the door handle.

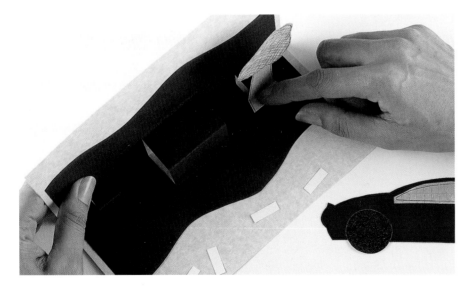

Tips
• Check the tree positions by using Blu-tack before gluing in place.

• If your trees will not fit inside the card, cut off the folded tab and create a second one – this will shorten the tree.

• Use a small bottle to bend the wire around when making the key ring.

7 Glue the black card inside the grey card – making sure the centre folds line up. Glue the trees to the left and right protruding boxes. Glue the car to the centre box. Punch three ½ cm (¼ in) circles from red card. Cut four tiny rectangles for from white scrap paper. Alternating red circles with white card, glue these in front of the car to create road markings.

▶ Front of card

8 Cut a strip of black card 21 × 3 cm (8¼ × 1⅛ in). Trim the long sides to give a wavy strip. Punch four ½ cm (¼ in) circles from red card. Cut four tiny rectangles from white scrap paper. Glue the pieces along the black strip.

9 Using the template on page 98 draw and cut the top of the key from black card. Draw and cut the bottom of the key from silver paper. Punch a tag from red card. Using the ½ cm (¼ in) punch, punch a circle at the top of the tag and top half of the key.

10 Bend the wire into a key ring – allowing the ends to overlap, and trim any excess wire. Thread the wire through the tag and key. Glue the key to the centre of the card to finish.

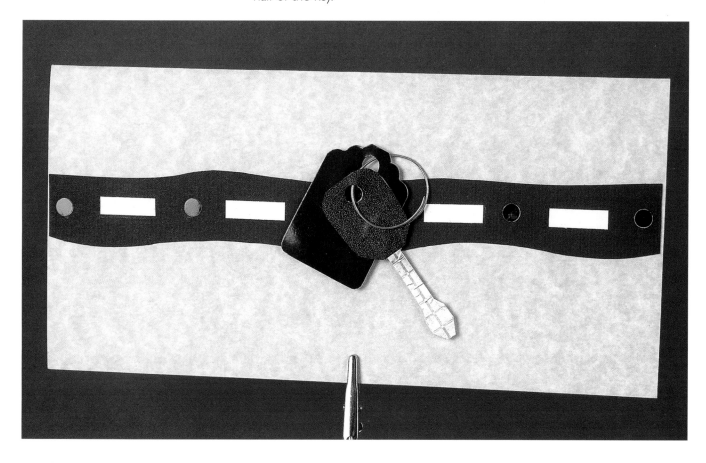

easter chick

difficulty
level ◆◆

Spring colours and a newly hatched chick: this card is fun for sending your Easter greetings. A great design for making with children – allowing them to characterize the features of the chick and personalize the card. Change the colour of the flowers and ribbon for a different look.

You will need

Paper/Card

▸ 210 x 297 mm (8½ x 11 in) white card

▸ 210 x 297 mm (8½ x 11 in) cream hand-made/textured paper

▸ 210 x 148 mm (8¼ x 5¾ in) papers in dark yellow, bright yellow, dark green and light green

▸ Paper scraps in black, white, and orange

Equipment

▸ Pencil

▸ Ruler

▸ Paper trimmer

▸ Bone folder

▸ Eraser

▸ Black marker

▸ Scissors

▸ ½ cm (¼ in) circle punch

▸ 1 cm (½ in) cm circle punch

▸ Glue stick

▸ Black ink pad

▸ Sand-coloured ink pad

▸ Medium daisy punch

▸ 12 cm (4¾ in) length of yellow ribbon

▸ 21 cm (8¼ in) length of yellow ribbon

▸ Clear sticky tape

▸ Sticky pads

▶ Inside of card

1 Measure and cut a piece of white card 19 x 19 cm (7½ x 7½ in) and fold in half to create the inner card. Measure and cut a piece of card 21 x 21 cm (8¼ x 8¼ in) and fold in half to create the outer card. On the inner card, draw a horizontal line 6.5 cm (2½ in) down from the top. With the main fold on the left, fold over the top corner of the card so it meets this line. Rub the bone folder across to give a neat crease.

2 Open back the fold. Open the card and tease the fold forward. Rub away all pencil lines.

3 Using the templates on page 101 and a black marker pen draw and cut out the chick and hair piece from dark yellow paper, leaving a thin yellow border as you cut. Cut a beak from orange paper. Punch two black and two white circles from paper with the 1 cm (½ in) punch.

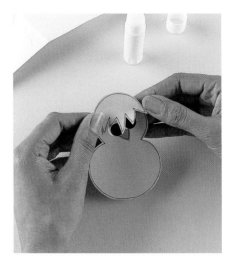

4 Glue the beak in place so the tip sits to the bottom of the head. Glue the eye pieces together and glue either side of the beak – allowing some of the beak to be hidden. Glue the hair piece so it sits partially over the eyes.

5 Using the templates on pages 100–101 cut out one nearly whole egg and two broken egg halves from handmade paper. Drag the sand-coloured inkpad over the raised areas of the shells. Drag the edges of the shells along the black inkpad. Glue a scrap of yellow paper behind the nearly whole egg, filling in the crack.

6 Using the daisy punch, punch four bright yellow, three dark yellow and two orange daisies. Using the ½ cm (¼ in) punch, punch circles from the same papers and glue onto the daisies so that the centre is a different colour from the daisy.

7 Draw and cut two dark and two light grass pieces from green paper using the template on page 101.

8 Position the chicken, egg shells and grass inside the card. Glue and position the top of the egg shell onto the left fold down flap – and ensuring that the the top shell meets the bottom shell and that the card folds easily. Once in place glue all the pieces and the grass to the card. Glue the daisies over the grass. Glue the outer card to the inner card to finish.

Front of card

9 Punch six daisies and circular centres and glue together as you did in step 6. Cut a length of yellow ribbon 25cm. Using the template on page 101 cut a dark and light piece of grass. Using the template on page 100 cut out the whole large egg and ink the edges and surface as you did in step 5. Cut another length of ribbon a bit longer than the width of the egg.

10 Glue the short ribbon across the egg and fix the ends to the back with sticky tape. Tie the long ribbon into a bow and stick to the left of the horizontal ribbon. Stick one of the daisies toward the right and end of the ribbon with a sticky pad.

11 Position and glue the egg 6 cm (2⅜ in) from the top of the card. Glue on the grass and flowers as you did in step 8 to finish.

Tip
• Use Blu-tack to position the pop-up egg shell before gluing in place.

• If using a pigment ink pad – heat with a heat tool to set before gluing the inked shell pieces to the card.

christmas baubles

A traditional Christmas colour scheme with a twist: the central hanging bauble is a lovely surprise, and makes this card a decoration in its own right. There's room to write a greeting in gold down the red panel on the front. But the inside is so special, you may want to write other messages on the back.

You will need

Paper/Card

▸ 210 x 297 mm (8½ x 11 in) cream cards

▸ 210 x 148 mm (8¼ x 5¾ in) cream card

▸ 210 x 297 mm (8½ x 11 in) red and gold papers

▸ Scrap dark green paper

Equipment

▸ Pencil

▸ Ruler

▸ Paper trimmer

▸ Bone folder

▸ Embossing tool

▸ Cutting mat

▸ Craft knife

▸ Scissors

▸ Glue stick

▸ Chestnut-coloured ink pad

▸ Tiny star punch

▸ 1 metre (1 yard) of gold thread

▸ 2.5 cm (1 in) circle punch

▸ Clear sticky tape

▶ Inside of card

1 Draw and cut a piece of cream card 21 x 21 cm (8¼ x 8¼ in) – the outer card. Draw vertical lines 1/2 cm (1/4 in) in from the edges down the left and right sides of the card. Cut the second piece of cream card 21 x 20 cm (8¼ x 7⅞ in) – the inner card. Using the embossing tool and bone folder, fold the outer card in half and leave to one side. Fold the inner card in half, then fold each half in half again outwards.

2 Open out the inner card. Place the large bauble template from page 102 across the centrefold and 5.5 cm (2⅛ in) down from the top and draw around it. Using the craft knife and cutting board cut out the bauble completely. Rub away all pencil marks.

3 Using the small-bauble template on page 102 draw and cut out two baubles from your remaining smaller sheet of cream card. Rub away pencil lines. Run the ink pad around the edges of the baubles and across the surface. Tear strips of gold, red and green papers. Glue the strips across the baubles at an angle – allowing some of the cream card to show above and below. Trim off any excess paper.

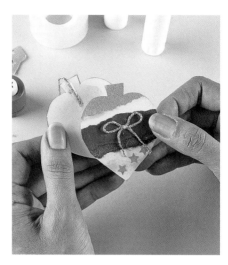

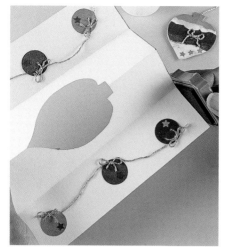

4 Tie two small bows from gold thread and glue in the centre of each bauble. Punch six tiny stars from gold paper, and glue three onto the bottom right of each bauble. Cut an 8 cm (3⅛ in) length of gold thread, and fix it behind one bauble with sticky tape. Glue both baubles back to back and leave to dry.

5 Using the circle punch, punch two each from the red, green and gold papers. Cut two 20 cm (8 in) lengths of gold thread. Tie six small bows. Punch two red, gold and green stars. Open out the inner card and position the threads along the side panels in a curving line. Glue the tiny baubles along the threads. Glue a bow and star to each bauble.

6 Ink the edges of the inner card. Fix the hanging bauble behind the centre fold with clear sticky tape, making sure it is hanging in the centre of the hole.

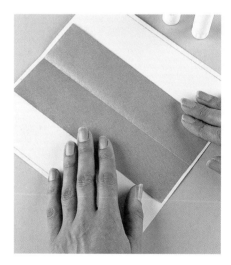

7 Cut a piece of gold paper 10 cm x 20 cm (3⅞ x 7⅞ in). Fold in half and glue across the inside centre fold of the outer card.

8 Using the pencil lines (that you drew on the outer card in step 1) as a guide, fix the inner card to the outer card with double-sided sticky tape. Gently rub away any pencil lines that still show.

▶ Front of card

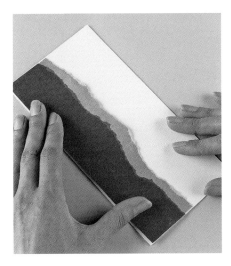

9 Cut a strip of red paper 21 x 4 cm (8¼ x 1⅝ in), then tear along one long edge. Cut a strip of gold paper 21 cm x 5 cm (8¼ x 2 in) and tear down one long edge. Glue the red strip on top of the gold strip leaving the torn gold edge showing. Glue the papers down the left-hand edge of the card. Make three small baubles as you did in step 5, and position them down the right-hand side of the card.

Tip
• Adapt this card for other occasions, by making the dangling bauble a flower, star, heart, or even cut-out numbers, and replace the smaller baubles with corresponding shapes. Such cards could then be sent as a thank-you card, Valentine or landmark birthday card, such as a 21st.

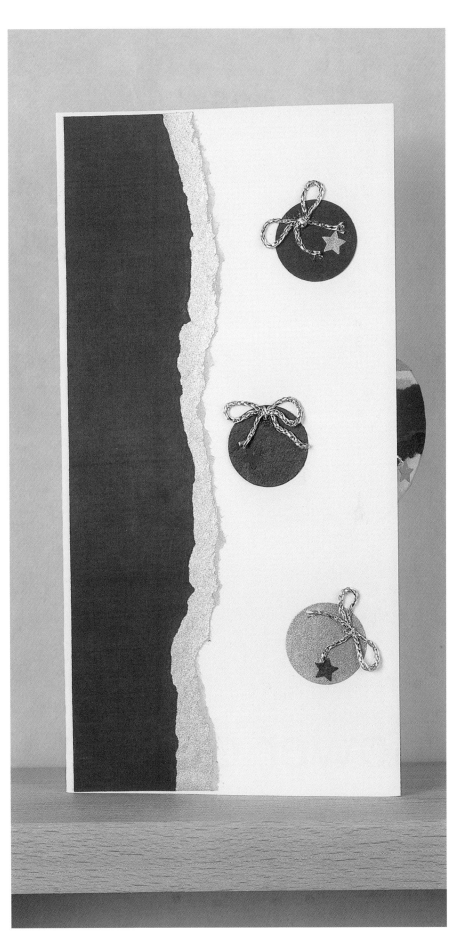

shower of gifts

difficulty
level ◆◆

Expanding on the idea of a baby shower where friends and family give gifts to an expectant mother, this card can be sent to shower someone with gifts on other occasions too. Use colours to match a wedding colour scheme or replace the gifts with baby items.

You will need

Paper/Card

- Two 210 x 297 mm (8½ x 11 in) white cards
- 210 x 297 mm (8½ x 11 in) pale blue paper
- Scrap coloured and patterned paper pieces: pale blue, pale lilac, patterned pink, pink stripe, glitter blue, shades of cream, glitter silver, darker blue, pearlescent magnolia, plain pink, silver, and claret

Equipment

- Silver marker pen
- Scissors
- Pencil
- Ruler
- Embossing tool
- Eraser
- Glue stick
- ½ cm (¼ in) circle punch
- 1 metre (1 yard) silver thread
- Sticky tape
- Clear embossing inkpad
- Embossing powders: lilac, pink and silver
- Heat tool
- Spotty rubber stamp
- Stars-and-swirl rubber stamp
- Approx 15 cm (6 in) lengths of thin ribbon in silver-grey, lilac, cream and pale blue
- Tiny heart punch

▶ Inside of card

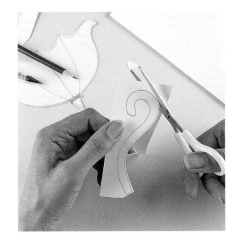 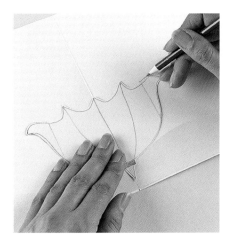

1 Fold one piece of white card in half and open out. Using the templates on page 103 and a silver marker pen, draw and cut out the open umbrella and handle from the second piece of white card, leaving a thin white border all round. Mark the fold lines in pencil on the umbrella. Draw silver lines to show the sections of the umbrella, and fill in a silver band around the base of the tip.

2 Cut a strip of pale blue paper 29 x 4 cm (11⅜ x 1⅝ in). Cut a wavy line across the top and glue the paper along the bottom of the card – leaving a slim white border on the very bottom. Fold along the centre line of the umbrella. Fold the side tabs forwards toward the centre fold. Rub away all pencil marks. Position the umbrella on the white card so that the folds sit together, 4 cm (1⅝ in) up from the bottom. Mark a faint pencil line around the side tabs.

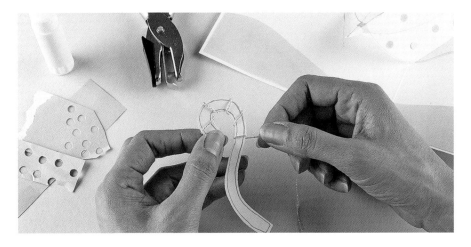

3 Punch tiny circles from pink and magnolia paper and glue them onto the umbrella. Cut a length of silver thread 33 cm (13 in). Wrap it around the handle and fix to the back with sticky tape.

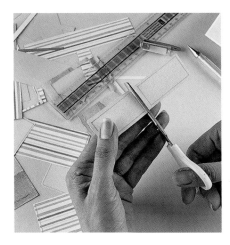

4 Using the templates on page 103 and a silver marker draw the gift shapes and cut them out leaving a thin white border: one square from plain lilac, pink-stripe and pink-print paper; one large rectangle from glittery blue, pale blue and pink-stripe paper; three small rectangles from shades of cream paper; and one small rectangle from blue paper.

5 Emboss the lilac square using the spotty stamp and lilac powder. Emboss the large blue rectangle using the star-and-swirl stamp and silver powder. Emboss one small rectangle using the spotty stamp and pink powder.

6 Punch one tiny heart from claret paper and one from silver paper. Glue the claret heart to the pink embossed gift, and the silver heart to a small rectangle. Tie the ribbon pieces into bows and stick on the gifts. Wrap a piece of silver thread around the embossed square so three lengths are visible at the front and fix at the back. Tie a silver-thread bow and fix onto this gift.

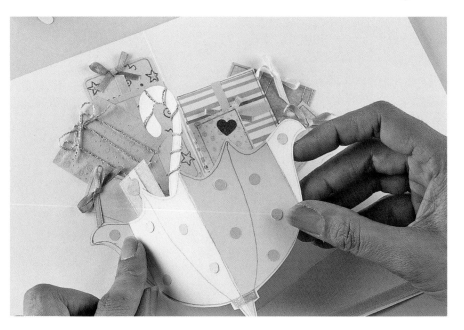

7 Glue the striped rectangle gift 6.5 cm (2½ in) up from the bottom of the card and to the left of the centre fold. Glue the glitter gift opposite on the right of the fold. Position, then glue the remaining parcels onto the card in layers, ensuring that they stay within the pencil lines you made in step 2.

8 Stick the two gifts with hearts onto the back of the umbrella, so they peep over the top. Glue the handle on the umbrella to the left of the centrefold. Rub away pencil marks.

Glue the umbrella onto the card using the pencil lines as a guide. Punch eight tiny hearts from blue paper and glue around the card. Stick the blue ribbon along the bottom of the card.

Front of card

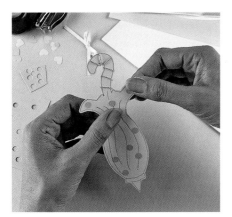

9 Using the template on page 103 and silver marker, draw and cut out the closed umbrella. Draw on the silver lines. Punch tiny circles from lilac and magnolia paper. Tie a cream bow. Wrap and fix silver thread round the handle. Punch ten tiny hearts from blue paper. Cut a wavy strip of pale blue paper the width of the card. Cut a strip of pale blue ribbon the width of the card.

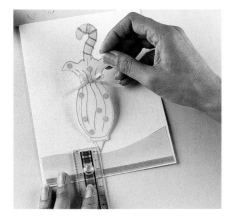

10 Glue the circles and bow onto the umbrella. Glue the blue wavy strip across the bottom of the card. Glue the blue ribbon over the bottom edge of the wavy strip. Position and glue the umbrella centrally on the front of the card, so that it sits just above the wavy strip. Glue hearts around the outside.

Tips

• Emboss the paper before drawing and cutting out the gifts, then save the spare paper for another project.

• Make the pieces for the front of the card at the same time as preparing the inner card pieces.

great news

difficulty
level ◆◆◆

Great news is a thrill to share and always a joy to hear. This design uses classic celebration motifs – champagne corks popping and party balloons. The central panel can be used to add a message such as "Congratulations", while the bottle labels can be used to write the recipients name and the name of the sender. This card would also be ideal for use as an invitation to a really special party.

You will need

Paper/Card

▶ 210 x 297 mm (8½ x 11 in) hammered white card

▶ Two 210 x 297 mm (8½ x 11 in) plain white cards

▶ 210 x 148 mm (8¼ x 5¾ in) beige card

▶ 210 x 148 mm (8¼ x 5¾ in) gold card

▶ 210 x 148 mm (8¼ x 5¾ in) yellow patterned paper

Equipment

▶ Pencil

▶ Paper trimmer

▶ Eraser

▶ Embossing tool

▶ Bone folder

▶ Craft knife

▶ Cutting mat

▶ Scissors

▶ Glue stick

▶ 1 cm (½ in) circle punch

▶ ½ cm (¼ in) circle punch

▶ 4 strips of gold Lametta (tinsel strips)

▶ Clear sticky tape

▶ 8 gold star sequins

▶ Red, lime green, yellow and lilac ink pads

▶ Balloon rubber stamp

▶ Star punch

▶ 1 metre (1 yard) gold thread

▶ Sticky pads

▶ Blu-tack

▶ Inside of card

1 Cut the hammered card 30 x 20 cm (12 x 8 in) – outer card. Cut one white card 30 x 20 cm (12 x 8 in) – inner card. Fold both in half. Using the template on page 104 draw and cut out the pop-up panel from white card and fold in half. Using the craft knife and cutting mat, cut along inner curved line. Erase pencil marks.

2 Using the embossing tool groove a line from the ends of the centre cut to the inner points underneath. Score a vertical line down the centre of the panel. While folding the template again – push the card under the curved cut backwards, and the card above forwards. Rub the bone folder over these creases.

3 Open out the white inner card and place the panel 4 cm (1⅝ in) down from the top and across the middle fold– making sure the folds sit neatly together. Mark four pencil dots on the inner card in the inner cut points of the tabs, at points A, B, C and D (see template). Using the craft knife and cutting mat cut a vertical line down either side – between the pencil marks. Rub away pencil marks.

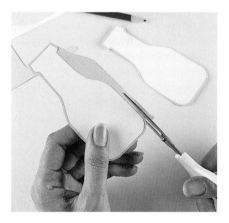

4 Using the template on page 104, draw and cut out two bottles from white card. Rub away pencil lines. Glue the white bottles to beige card and cut them out – leaving a slim beige border.

5 Cut two strips of beige card 6.5 × 3 cm (2½ × 1⅛ in). Rub away pencil lines. Place the strips under the bottles at the necklines. Fold the left side over the bottle and fold down the top corner. Fold the right side over the bottle and fold down the top corner. Remove from the bottles and trim any excess from along the bottom.

6 Cut two strips of gold card roughly 0.5 cm (¼ in) thick and to fit across the bottle. Punch two gold circles using the 1 cm (½ in) circle punch. Punch two beige circles using the ½ cm (¼ in) circle punch. Glue the small circles onto the large circles. Glue the large circles onto the gold strips. Leave to dry.

7 Cut two 3 × 3 cm (1⅛ × 1⅛ in) pieces of white card. Glue them to beige card and cut out leaving a slim beige border. Glue the collars onto the bottles. Glue the gold strips below the collars and trim off any excess. Glue the labels onto the bottles.

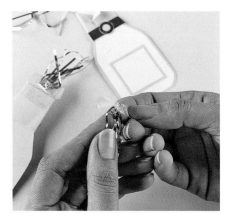

8 Cut two strips of Lametta into four smaller strips. Bunch up and wrap the end with sticky tape. Glue the Lametta onto the back of the bottles behind the pouring rim. Trim to roughly 5 cm (2 in) in length.

9 Ink and stamp one red, lime green, yellow and lilac balloon on white card. Cut out the balloons leaving a slim white border all round. Punch four stars from the patterned paper. Cut four lengths of gold thread roughly 7 cm (1¾ in). Glue the stars onto the balloons. Fix the threads behind each balloon.

10 Using the templates on page 104, draw and cut two corks from beige card. Stick a very thin strip of gold card at the neck of each cork. Trim off excess. Using the template draw and cut two starbursts from gold card.

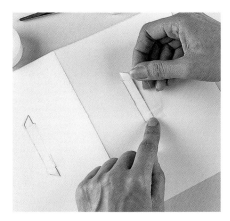

11 Push the side tabs on the centre panel into the cuts on the inner card. Fix the tabs behind the card with clear sticky tape. Glue the inner card to the outer card.

12 Glue the starbursts either side of the panel. Glue the corks above the starbursts. Glue a star sequin either side of each cork and one on the cork. Glue the balloons to the bottom left and right. Run the balloon strings over the glue stick, and stick them down in a curvy line. Trim if needed. Glue a star sequin to each bottle label.

13 Position the bottles on the ends of the bottom sections of the panel. Use Blue-tack to test that the card closes easily with the bottles inside. Then glue the bottles in place.

▶ Front of card

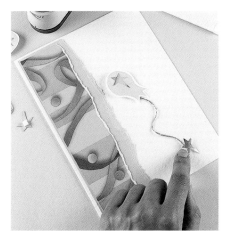

14 Make two balloons as you did in step 9. Cut a piece of the patterned paper 5 × 19 cm (2 × 7½ in) and tear down one long side. Glue this onto a piece of the beige paper, leaving a thin beige border on the straight edge. Tear the beige paper along the torn edge, about 1 cm (½ in) out from the torn patterned edge.

15 Glue the beige and patterned panel along the left side of the card. Fix the balloons onto the right side of the card with sticky pads. Trim the balloon strings as needed. Punch a gold star and fix to the bottom of the threads using a sticky pad. Then fix to the card.

Tips
• Slightly curl the Lametta by running the blade of the scissors along the loose ends. If the curl is too tight, run the blade along the underside to straighten and repeat with less pressure.

• Make a balloon stamp by cutting a balloon from thin foam and gluing it to a piece of plastic or wood.

oh christmas tree!

difficulty
level ◆

The family Christmas tree plays an important role in celebrations at this festive time so what better theme to use for a specially designed card. Here I've used fresh and contemporary blue and white shades, but the colour scheme can be changed to the more traditional Christmas colours of red, green and gold if preferred.

You will need

Paper/Card

▸ 210 x 297 mm (8½ x 11 in) pale blue card

▸ Two 210 x 297 mm (8½ x 11 in) white glitter cards

▸ 210 x 148 mm (8¼ x 5¾ in) white card

Equipment

▸ Pencil

▸ Ruler

▸ Eraser

▸ Embossing tool

▸ Bone folder

▸ Paper trimmer

▸ Scissors

▸ Glue stick

▸ 40 cm (15 ¾ in) length of silver thread

▸ 9 white and 18 blue seed beads

▸ Clear sticky tape

▸ 1mm hole punch

▸ 1 cm (½ in) circle punch

▸ ½ cm (¼ in) circle punch

▸ Glitter glue

▸ Sticky pad

Inside of card

1 Measure and cut a piece of blue card 27 x 13.5 cm (10⅝ x 5¼ in). Groove and fold using the embossing tool and bone folder. Using the template on page 102, cut out three trees in white glitter card.

2 Fold all the trees in half with the glittery side of the trees on the inside, then open out. (Glitter card is usually plain on the back). Glue the back of the right side of one tree to the back of the left side of the second tree. Glue the back of the right side of the second tree to the back of the left side of the third tree.

3 Using the 1mm hand punch, punch three holes in each section of the tree, varying the positions. Harden one end of the silver thread with glue to make threading easier. Starting from the back and top of the tree, weave the silver thread through the first hole, add a blue, white and blue bead, thread through the next hole, add three more beads, and so on, until you come out of the bottom hole at the back. Trim the thread and secure at the back with sticky tape.

4 Punch 27 small circles from the left-over blue card. Punch 12 larger circles from white card. Draw and cut a length of white card to fit all the way across the top of the inside of the card, in the shape of dripping icicles.

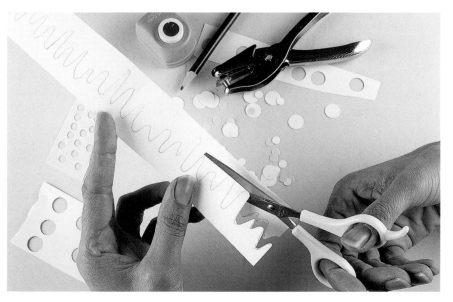

5 Glue the icicle strip across the top of the card. Glue seven small blue circles randomly over the strip. Place the tree in the middle of the card and lightly pencil round the outline. Glue the white circle snowflakes randomly around the outer edges of the card. Apply dots of glitter glue between the large circles. Glue the remaining blue circles randomly onto the tree branches. Glue the tree in the centre of the card.

Front of card

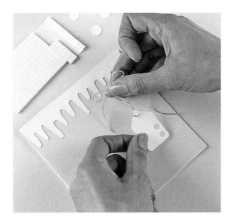

Tip
• When gluing the tree together do not worry if the edges are not perfectly aligned – slight differences will create a more realistic 3D effect.

6 Cut a second strip of white icicles the width of the card front. Punch seven large white circles and two small blue circles. Using the template on page 102 cut out a small tag. Thread the tag onto silver thread and tie a bow.

7 Glue the icicle strip across the top of the card. Glue two blue circles to the bottom right of the tag. Glue the bow at the top of the tag on the end of an icicle, and fix the tag with sticky pads. Glue the snowflakes around the remaining area.

birthday surprise

difficulty
level ◆◆◆
A traditional jack-in-the-box is probably the ultimate "pop-up" toy! This is a really fun and cheerful card to send for a child's birthday greeting, or as an invitation to their birthday party. You can add a number to the box to specify their age.

You will need

Paper/Card

▸ 210 x 297 mm (8½ x 11 in) red card

▸ 210 x 297 mm (8½ x 11 in) blue card

▸ 210 x 148 mm (8¼ x 5¾ in) yellow card

▸ 210 x 148 mm (8¼ x 5¾ in) white card

▸ Paper scraps: green, pink and orange

▸ Scrap silver card

Equipment

▸ Pencil

▸ Ruler

▸ Eraser

▸ Paper trimmer

▸ Embossing tool

▸ Bone folder

▸ Black marker pen

▸ Scissors

▸ 2.5 cm (1 in) circle punch

▸ 1 cm (½ in) circle punch

▸ Tiny star-shaped hand punch

▸ Double-sided sticky tape

▸ Tiny flower-shaped hand punch

▸ Fibre-tip pens: orange, red, green, yellow and black

▸ 1 metre (1 yard) silver thread

▸ Medium star punch

▸ Small sticky pads

▸ Glue stick

▸ 20 cm (8 in) length white and silver ribbon

▸ Silver ink pad

▸ Silver glitter glue

▸ Clear sticky tape

▸ Inside of card

1 Measure and cut a piece of red card 21 x 21 cm (8¼ x 8¼ in). Groove down the centre with the embossing tool and fold using the bone folder. Rub away pencil marks. Using the template on page 105 draw the outline of the box in black pen on blue card and cut it out. Add the other black lines as per the template, and score the lines with the embossing tool, ready for folding.

2 Punch two 2.5 cm (1 in) circles from yellow paper. Punch two 1 cm (½ in) circles each from red, pink, yellow and green paper. Punch three tiny stars from orange paper. Glue in place on the two centre sections of the box. Add dots of glitter glue over the box and leave to dry.

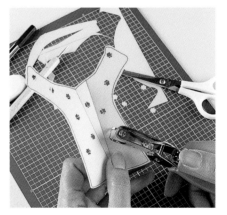

3 Apply glue to the tab of the blue box. Press the ends together to complete the box.

4 Using the template on page 106 and black marker pen draw the body on yellow card and cut out. Using a pencil, mark the fold lines and score along them with the embossing tool. Punch tiny flowers through the body using the hand punch. Rub away the pencil lines.

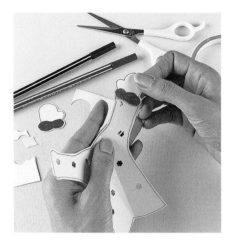

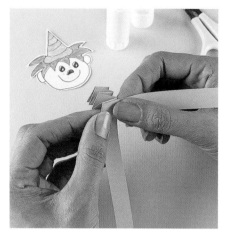

5 Using the templates on page 106 and black marker pen, draw and cut out two mittens, remembering to turn one over to give you a right and left mitten. Using the red fibre-tip pen colour in the mitten trim. Stick the mittens to the ends of the arms on the front using double-sided sticky tape.

6 Using the template on page 106 cut out the head from white card. Colour in the hat, nose and hair using fibre-tip pens. Cut three lengths of silver thread 10 cm (3⅞ in). Punch four stars from silver paper. Fix a sticky pad to the back of three stars. Stick the end of the threads onto each sticky pad.

7 Cut two 9 x 1.5 cm (3½ x ⅝ in) strips of pink and orange paper from scrap pieces. Position two ends at right angles and glue together. Fold one piece over the other and continue to fold to make a concertina spring. Trim any excess and glue the ends together to complete the spring.

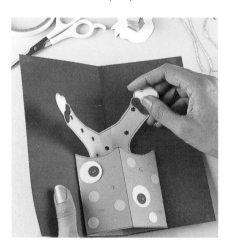

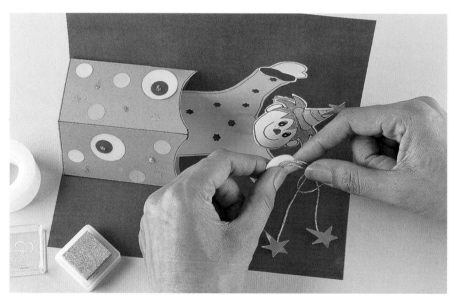

8 Fix the box across the bottom centre of the card with double-sided sticky tape. Fix the body inside the box in the same way – ensuring the centre fold of the body sits nicely against the fold of the card. Glue one star to the top of the clown's hat. Stick the "spring" on the back of the clown's head, and then fix it to the card, so that it sits just at the top of the body.

9 Fix the three threaded stars in place on the card with the sticky pads. Fix the loose ends of thread behind the left hand with sticky tape – allowing the threads to sit up loose above the card. Run the silver inkpad along the front fold of the box.

Front of card

10 Cut two strips from yellow card 10 × 2 cm (3⅞ × ¾ in). Cut two more strips from orange and blue paper the same size. Punch tiny stars on the yellow strips. Glue the coloured strips behind the yellow strips.

11 Make three stars on strings the same as you did in step 6. Cut a length of ribbon 15 cm (5⅞ in). Tie the ribbon into a bow.

12 Glue the coloured strips along the top and bottom of the card. Fix the tail strings of the stars to the card by gluing the bow over the top of them. Peel off the sticky pads behind each star and stick down, making sure that the strings are loose.

Tips

• Try to get an even distribution of the tiny stars on the coloured strips on the front of the card.

• Experiment with different patterns for "Jack's" box: stripes, zigzags, or checks.

• You could substitute the silver stars for balloons, using the balloon stamp from the Great News card, pages 60–3.

baby wash day

Tiny clothes on a washing line are enough to
make your heart melt, and something proud new parents will be
generating for real very soon! Use the appropriate colours for a boy or girl.
This card can also be adapted for twins or triplets etc by hanging one, two or
three baby-grows on the washing line.

You will need

Paper/Card

▸ 210 x 297 mm (8½ x 11 in) white card

▸ 210 x 297 mm (8½ x 11 in) green paper

▸ 210 x 297 mm (8½ x 11 in) blue paper

▸ 210 x 148 mm (8¼ x 5¾ in) peach card

▸ Coloured and patterned card scraps: peach, green, blue, yellow and red

▸ Scrap yellow glitter card

Equipment

▸ Ruler

▸ Pencil

▸ Eraser

▸ Cutting mat

▸ Paper trimmer

▸ Embossing tool

▸ Bone folder

▸ Scissors

▸ Black marker pen

▸ ½ cm (¼ in) circle punch

▸ 1 cm (½ in) circle punch

▸ Clear sticky tape

▸ Glue stick

▸ Scraps of yellow and pink thread

▸ Double-sided sticky tape

▸ Small sticky pads

▸ 33 cm (13 in) length black thread

▸ 5 yellow paper clips

▸ 1 cm (½ in) square punch

▸ Safety pin, yellow button, and tiny pink brad

▸ 33 cm (13 in) length thin pink ribbon

▶ Inside of card

1 Measure and cut a piece of white card 28 x 21 cm (11 x 8¼ in). Mark a vertical line 7 cm (2¾ in) in from both short sides of the card. Groove and fold along these lines. Rub away all pencil marks. Using a pencil and the template on page 107 draw and cut two washing posts from peach card. Go over the inner three lines and the top in black pen, leaving the side tabs in pencil. Score along the vertical lines and cut out the posts.

2 Using the templates on page 108 and black marker pen draw and cut the items of clothing from the selection of coloured and patterned card. Using the ½ cm (¼ in) punch, punch three pink circles and glue to the baby suit then two lilac circles to the hat. Add dots and crosses with the black marker to illustrate buttons.

3 Draw and cut a strip of blue paper to be the sky, slightly smaller than the width of the whole card,

Cut a wavy line along one length. Cut out the grass template on page 107 using green paper.

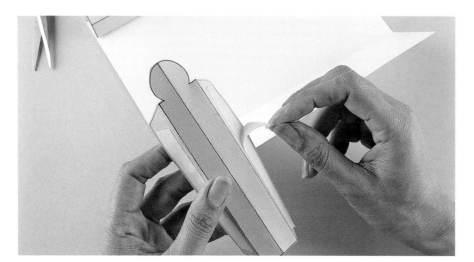

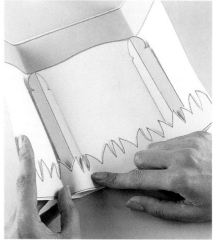

4 Fix a strip of double-sided sticky tape to each of the two outer panels on the posts. (Make sure you do all this step without peeling off the backing first, so that you can check that the posts allow the card to open out enough. Only then peel off the backing and fix the posts for real.) Position one post to the right of the left fold in the card – slightly higher than the bottom of the card. Bring the left side panel up to meet it, so both sides stick across the fold. Repeat for the other post. When the card panels are opened – the post should sit nearly in the folds.

5 Glue the blue sky across the top of the card. Glue the grass along the bottom, allowing it to sit over the bottom of the posts.

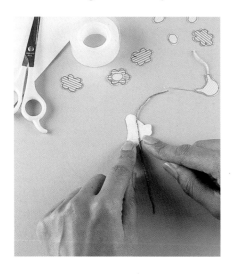

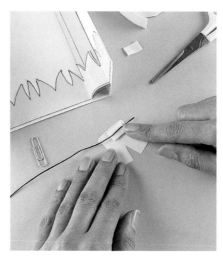

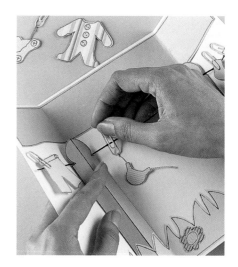

6 Cut a length of yellow thread and stick across the back of the bib. Cut a length of pink thread and fix to the hat with clear sticky tape. Using the templates on page 108 and black marker pen, draw and cut out four flowers and flower centres from patterned paper and glue together to make four complete flowers. Stick them across the grass.

7 Fix a piece of sticky foam to the back of the trousers. Secure one end of the black thread onto the foam and fix the trousers to the left panel of the card. Push a paper clip onto the trousers.

8 Sit the black thread behind the posts. Secure the boots to the opposite end of the thread in the same way as the trousers, and trim off any excess thread. Push a paper clip onto the baby-grow, bib and hat and secure them onto the middle section of the washing line – the line should be loose enough to enable the card to open and close freely.

▶ Front of card

9 Punch a square from each of the green, pink and yellow scraps of card and paper. Glue the button onto the pink square. Make up a flower as you did in step 6 and glue it onto the yellow square. Punch a ½ cm (¼ in) circle from the glitter card. Push the brad through the centre of the glitter circle and then through the hole in the head of the safety pin and fold back the tabs of the brad. Glue this to the green square. Allow to dry.

10 Glue the squares to the left side of the card front. Tie the pink ribbon around the card and make a knot. The ribbon can then be slipped on and off – to view the inside.

Tips
• Replace the paper clips with tiny wooden pegs. But remember, this will make the card bulkier, and you will need a box envelope.

• If you have found patterned paper rather than card for the clothing, glue it to scrap white card before cutting out the shapes.

▶ Variation *Twin boys*

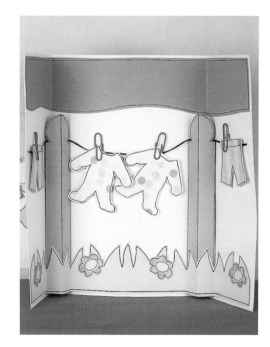

graduation day

difficulty level ◆◆◆ Attending a graduation ceremony is a proud moment for parents, family and friends, and of course, the graduates themselves! This free-standing design captures the event with stage and curtains, a mortar board and a diploma. This card could be enlarged to any size should you wish to embellish it further to make it a keepsake and present it in a box.

You will need

Paper/Card

▶ 210 x 297 mm (8½ x 11 in) cream card

▶ 210 x 148 mm (8¼ x 5¾ in) red and gold papers

▶ 210 x 148 mm (8¼ x 5¾ in) red tissue paper

▶ Scrap gold card

▶ Scrap cream paper

▶ Scrap red tissue paper

Equipment

▶ Pencil

▶ Ruler

▶ Paper trimmer

▶ Craft knife

▶ Cutting mat

▶ Embossing tool

▶ Bone finder

▶ Eraser

▶ Glue stick

▶ Scissors

▶ Gold ink pad

▶ 28 cm (11 in) gold thread

▶ Chestnut ink pad

▶ 33 cm (13 in) red thread

▶ Scrap black foam

▶ Double-sided sticky tape

▶ 15 cm (5⅞ in) black thread

▶ Clear drying glue

▶ Gold star sequin

▶ Scrap red card

▶ Two red star sequins

▶ Inside of card

1 Cut a piece of cream card 21 x 24 cm (8½ x 9½ in). Then, following the measurements on the template on page 109, draw on all the lines. Using the craft knife and cutting mat, cut the card in half along the central vertical line. Leave the outer card to one side. On the inner card, cut along the four short vertical lines.

2 Using the embossing tool groove then fold this cut piece of card upwards along the second horizontal line down, downwards along the third horizontal line and upwards along the fourth horizontal line. The cut sections should sit up away from the main card when folded. Rub the bone folder along the folds, and erase all pencil marks.

3 Using the template on page 109 cut two curtains from red paper – remember to turn one over to give a right and left curtain. Cut two pieces of red tissue paper slightly larger that the curtains. Apply glue to the card and secure the tissue all over, scrunching the tissue to form creases on the surface. Trim away any excess tissue.

4 Ink the edges of each curtain with the gold ink pad. Rub the ink pad gently over the surface of the curtains so that the creases catch the gold ink. Leave to dry.

5 Cut two lengths of gold thread 15 cm (5⅞ in). Wrap each length twice around each curtain, tie into a knot and trim any excess.

6 Cut a 1.5 x 5.5 cm (¾ x 2¼ in) rectangle to be the diploma and snip the ends to give them a slight curve. Ink the edges using the chestnut ink pad, allowing the ink to seep over the front. Wind the red thread around the diploma and tie in a bow.

7 Cut out a mortar board hat from black foam, using scissors and the template on page 107. Double up the black thread twice and make a knot in the centre. Cut the folded ends and glue onto the top centre of the hat. Trim any excess.

8 Using the templates on page 108 and 109 draw and cut a curtain pelmet from gold card and the book from cream paper. Ink the edges of the book with chestnut ink. Fold in half and ink the fold. Gently press ink over the surface of the book to give it texture. Glue the gold star sequin to the top left of the book.

9 Take the piece of cream card that you set to one side in step 1 – this is the outer card. Fold this piece of card along the second line down and open back out. Cut a piece of gold paper 8 x 11 cm (3⅛ x 4⅜ in). Glue the gold paper over the fold so the top of the gold paper lines up with the top line. Now ink the edges of the inner card with gold ink and leave to dry.

10 Stick the inner card onto the outer card. Glue the curtains to the top of the card. Glue the shiny gold pelmet across the top of the curtains, leaving a slim cream border. Fix the mortar board to the top pop-out using double-sided sticky tape. Fix the diploma to the lower pop-out in the same way. Glue the book across the bottom of the card.

Back of card

11 Using the templates on page 108 and 109 draw and cut a second pelmet from gold card, and a stand from red card. Rub away all pencil marks. Fold the stand along the inner lines and open out. Drag the edges of the stand in the gold ink pad. Glue the pelmet across the top of the card back. Glue the middle of the stand to the centre bottom of the card and glue the star sequins in place.

Tips

• Water-based ink pads dry quickly and allow you to continue working straight away. If using pigment inks leave your work over night to avoid smudges.

• Check your measurements before cutting into the card to avoid having a bad fit and needing to start over.

wedding bows

difficulty
level ◆◆◆ For that special golden wedding anniversary, creating a hand-made
card with the style and finish that befits the occasion can sometimes
be a challenge, but this card certainly fits the bill. The colour scheme can be
changed and the bows replaced with other symbols, such as bells or horseshoes,
to make a wedding card. In cream and red it can even be a Valentine card.

You will need

Paper/Card

▸ Two 210 x 297 mm (8½ x 11 in) cream cards

▸ 210 x 297 mm (8½ x 11 in) copper-coloured paper

▸ 210 x 297 mm (8½ x 11 in) cream-pearl paper

▸ Scrap stone-coloured paper

Equipment

▸ Pencil

▸ Ruler

▸ Paper trimmer

▸ Scissors

▸ Embossing tool

▸ Bone folder

▸ Eraser

▸ Craft knife

▸ Cutting mat

▸ Tiny heart punch

▸ 40 cm (15 ¾ inch) length of brown ribbon

▸ Glue stick

▸ Clear drying glue

▸ Double sided sticky tape

▸ Scrap transluscent cream ribbon

▸ 2 copper brads

▸ Small sticky pads

▶ Inside of card

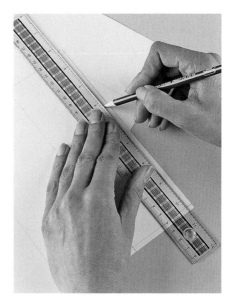

1 Measure and cut two pieces of cream card 28 x 21 cm (11 x 8¼ in). On both pieces, and with the longer sides forming the top and bottom edges, draw vertical lines down the card at 7 cm (2¾ in), 14 cm (5 ½ in) 21 cm (8¼ in) on both pieces. (You may find it easier to make pencil marks along the top and bottom edges and then join these up.) On one piece measure and mark a ½ cm (¼ in) line around all four sides – this will be the inner card.

2 Using the paper trimmer cut away the ½ cm (¼ in) border on the inner piece of card. Using the embossing tool and bone folder, groove and fold both pieces of card along the centre line. Fold up each of the side panels so the ends of the card sit close to the middle fold. Open out and rub away all pencil lines. Run the bone folder along the folds to give neat creases. You should now have two pieces of folded card – the inner smaller piece and the outer, slightly larger piece.

▶ Tips

• Test the craft knife on scrap card before the real project materials. This helps you past the initial, error-causing hesitation of using a knife.

• When cutting around the bows and hearts, take it slowly, and steady your hand by resting your little finger on the surface you are using.

• When positioning and piercing brads – place a scrap piece of foam underneath to ensure a neat finish.

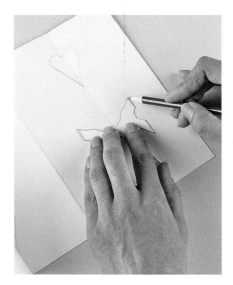

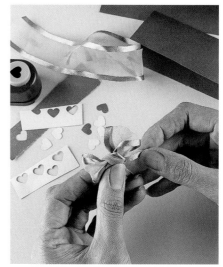

3 Place the bow template (from page 110) over the left fold, 4 cm (1⅝ in) down from the top of the card. Draw round in pencil. Repeat on the right, with 8cm (3⅛ in) between the bottom of the card and the bottom of the knot. Repeat with the heart, positioning it 6cm (2⅜ in) from the bottom of the left fold and 3cm (1⅛ in) down from the top of the right.

4 Using the craft knife and cutting mat carefully cut out the shapes, but leave the card intact where indicated on the cutting templates on page 110. Rub away all pencil lines. Gently tease the cut areas forwards while folding the card back.

5 Cut two pieces of copper-coloured paper 18 x 11 cm (7⅛ x 4⅜ in) and fold in half. Punch two hearts from copper-coloured paper. Punch six hearts from stone coloured paper. Cut two lengths of brown ribbon 24 cm (9½ in) and tie into bows.

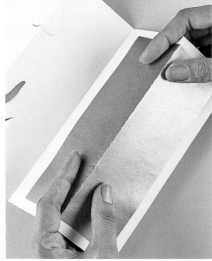

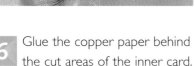

6 Glue the copper paper behind the cut areas of the inner card.

7 Stick the inner card to the outer card. Glue the little copper hearts to the cut-out card hearts. Glue the stone-coloured hearts around the edges of the card. Glue the ribbons over the pop-out card bows – using clear-drying glue. Make sure you use sufficient glue and manipulate the ribbon carefully so that the bows sit neatly on the cut-out bows. Trim off excess.

Front of card

8 Tear a piece of cream pearl paper roughly 10 x 4 cm (3⅞ x 1⅝ in). Tear a piece of copper-coloured paper roughly 7 x 3 cm (2¾ x 1⅛ in) and glue on top of the pearl paper. Punch a stone-coloured heart and glue on top. Cut a piece of cream transluscent ribbon 13 cm (5⅛ in) in length and fix to the papers using the tiny brads. Fix the panel to the card with sticky pads. Use the template on page 110 to make a matching box envelope.

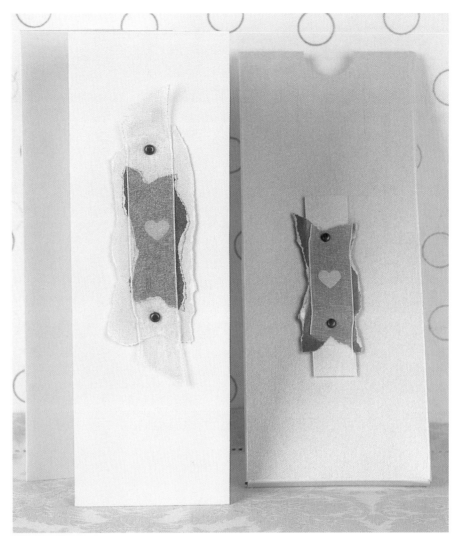

Variation

This variation shows a different decorative panel on the front of the card, and a different colour scheme that would make this card suitable for giving as a wedding card.

birthday butterflies

difficulty level ◆

A lovely fresh and contemporary looking card, in which butterflies miraculously seem to flutter out of the card when you open it. This is achieved by the clever use of transparent acetate across the centre of the card. As with most of the cards in this book, this design too can be adapted to incorporate other motifs or to suit a variety of occasions.

You will need

Paper/Card/Acetate

▸ 210 x 297 mm (8½ x 11 in)
   white card

▸ 210 x 148 mm (8¼ x 5¾ in)
   brightly coloured papers: yellow,
   lime green, pink, pale blue

▸ 210 x 148 mm (8¼ x 5¾ in)
   piece of clear acetate

▸ Scrap white card

Equipment

▸ Pencil

▸ Ruler

▸ Paper trimmer

▸ Eraser

▸ Grid stamp

▸ Ink pads: lilac, lemon yellow,
   and petal pink

▸ Spotty stamp

▸ 1 cm (½ in) circle punch

▸ Scissors

▸ Silver marker pen

▸ Silver peel-off butterflies

▸ Blue "stitch" ribbon

▸ Bone folder

▸ Glue stick

▸ Double-sided sticky tape

▸ 40 cm (15¾ in) silver thread

▶ Inside of card

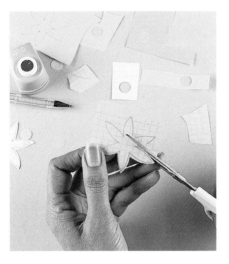

1 Measure and cut a piece of white card 21 x 15 cm (8¼ x 5⅞ in). Score with the embossing tool, fold in half and rub away pencil marks. Ink the grid stamp with lilac ink and stamp onto yellow paper. Ink again and stamp onto green paper. Ink the spotty stamp with yellow ink and stamp onto pink paper. Ink the spotty stamp with lilac and stamp onto blue paper.

2 Punch five circles from the coloured papers: two pink, one green stamped and one from the remaining colour. Cut five 12 x ½ cm (4¾ x ¼ in) strips of green paper for the stems. Draw in pencil four flowers from stamped papers: two yellow and one of each other colour. Go over the outlines in silver pen, then cut out, leaving a small border outside the line of the silver pen.

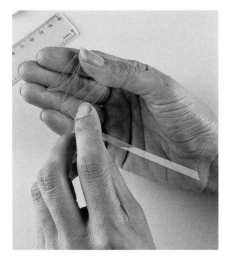

3 Peel off seven of the silver butterflies and stick them to a variety of coloured papers. Cut them out leaving a thin coloured border round the edge.

4 Cut a strip of acetate 1.5 x 25 cm (⅝ x 9⅞ in). Fold at 2 cm (¾ in) intervals along the strip into a zigzag. Once you have eight 2cm (¾ in) sections cut off the excess acetate.

5 Glue a different coloured circle to the centre of each of the four flowers. Glue the green stems behind each flower, and then position the two taller flowers either side of the centre fold of the card. Trip off any excess stems as required.

6 Fix a piece of double-sided sticky tape to the end sections of the acetate. Position the acetate 7 cm (2¾ in) up from the bottom and 1 cm (½ in) in from the left side of the card. Ensure the acetate goes horizontally across the card, then fix in place on the other side.

7 Glue the remaining two shorter flowers onto the card, ensuring that the flower heads are glued over the acetate ends. Trim off the stems as required.

8 Fix double-sided sticky tape to the back of the butterflies. Fix one end of silver thread to the back of a butterfly and glue to the left of the blue flower. Leaving some loose thread in between, fix the next, different-coloured butterfly to the silver thread and secure both onto the acetate. Continue to fix the

butterflies and thread across the acetate zigzag – until the acetate holds four butterflies. Fix the end of the thread to the back of a butterfly and secure onto the card above the far right flower. Stick the remaining butterfly between the two flowers on the left side of the card using double-sided sticky tape.

9 Cut a length of blue ribbon slightly longer than the width of the open card. Ink a piece of white card using the spotty stamp and lilac ink. Punch four circles from this stamped card. Glue the ribbon across the bottom of the card, then glue a circle on top of the ribbon at the end of each stem. Trim off any excess ribbon.

Front of card

10 Using the stamped white card from step 9, cut a piece 9.5 × 4.5 cm (3¾ × 1¾ in). Cut a wavy line along one side. Cut a length of blue ribbon 9.5 cm (3¾ in). Glue the ribbon to the stamped card.

11 Make up a flower as you did in step 5 and glue it 3 cm (1⅜ in) down from the top of the card. Trim the stem and glue the card-and-ribbon panel from step 10 over the top to finish.

Tips

• Use tweezers to peel the butterflies off their backing sheet to avoid bending or breaking them.

• When drawing your flowers, ensure there is enough paper around the edges for cutting out.

• When cutting with scissors, turn the paper around the scissors, not the scissors round the paper – this makes cutting easier, and makes for a smoother finish.

Variation

time to sow

difficulty
level ◆◆◆ A well-earned retirement can involve travelling, pursuing neglected hobbies, or relaxing days in the garden. This card focuses on those who enjoy their garden and all things floral.

You will need

Paper/Card

- 210 x 297 mm (8½ x 11 in) white card
- 210 x 297 mm (8½ x 11 in) green card
- 210 x 148 mm (8¼ x 5¾ in) sheets of brown, pale green, dark green and patterned green card
- Scrap papers: red, yellow, orange, shades of brown, mustard, checked, cream and cherry papers

Equipment

- Pencil
- Ruler
- Eraser
- Paper trimmer
- Embossing tool
- Bone folder
- Black marker pen
- Scissors
- Double-sided sticky tape
- Cocoa, chestnuut and black coloured ink pads
- 1 cm (½ in) circle punch
- ½ cm (¼ in) circle punch
- Tiny leaf punch
- Tiny pot punch
- Flower punches in three or four different sizes and shapes
- Rubber stamps – grid pattern and various garden tools
- 40 cm (15¾ in) length thin string
- Sticky tape
- Brown fibre-tip pen
- Glue stick
- Sticky pads

▶ Inside of card

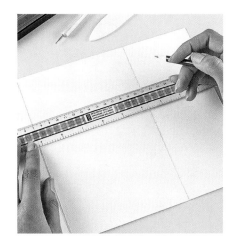

1 With the white card horizontally in front of you, draw vertical lines at 7 cm (2¾ in) and 21 cm (8¼ in). Score and fold along these lines to create the side flaps, which should overlap each other when closed.

2 Draw and cut two tree trunks from brown paper using the template on page 111. Score and fold along the lines. Glue along the length of one end and fix together to form square tubes.

3 Using the template on page 111, draw and cut 10 palm leaves from the dark and light green card. You will need five bending to the right and five bending to the left, so you can simply turn five over. Rub away pencil marks. Cut a wavy strip of pattered green paper to fit across the whole open width of the card.

4 Using the black marker pen and template on page 111, draw and cut out the hammock from beige card. Ink the grid stamp with chestnut ink and lightly stamp onto the hammock. Ink around the bottom edges of the hammock – allowing ink to cover the bottom areas.

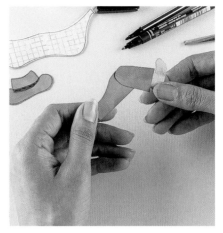

5 Cut two lengths of string roughly 8 cm (3 in) long. Fix one at each end of the hammock using sticky tape.

6 Using the templates on page 111 and black marker pen draw and cut a hat and the leg pieces from brown card and a foot from cream card.

7 Colour in the hat band with the brown marker. Ink the hat, leg and foot using chestnut ink. Glue the leg pieces together as shown above.

8 Glue the trunks into the folds of the card. Glue four palm leaves onto the top of each trunk, two facing out, two facing in.

9 Stick the hat onto the front of the hammock edge. Stick the leg to the hammock so that it crosses over from back to front at the knee. Using sticky tape, fix the ends of the hammock strings to the back of the remaining two palm leaves. Leave this completed hammock piece to one side.

10 Using the templates on page 111 cut three lipped pots from brown paper, two large pots from mustard paper and two small pots from checked paper. Ink the edges of each pot with the cocoa ink pad.

Tips
• Check the positioning of the tree trunks before securing in place.

• Use thin paper for the tree trunks to allow for easier folding.

▶ Front of card

11 Punch and draw a selection of leaves and foliage shapes from green paper, and a selection of flowers from different papers. Punch circles for the flower centres.

12 Glue the green strip across the bottom of the card. Glue the made-up flowers and pots along the bottom. Finally fix the hammock piece in place by securing the palm leaves on the ends of the strings to the top of the tree trunks with double-sided sticky tape.

13 Punch and cut out a further selection of flower pots and foliage, using the photograph below as a guide. Stamp the garden tools onto brown paper, using partial cocoa and partial black ink and cut out. Make up a second hat.

14 Cut out two more wavy green strips for the grass, and glue across the bottom of each front panel. Finally glue the other items onto the front panels of the card, trying out the arrangement before gluing.

BABY CARRIAGE
pages 16–19

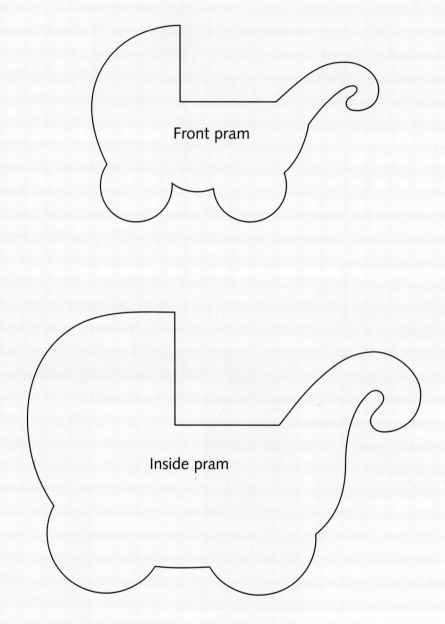

Front pram

Inside pram

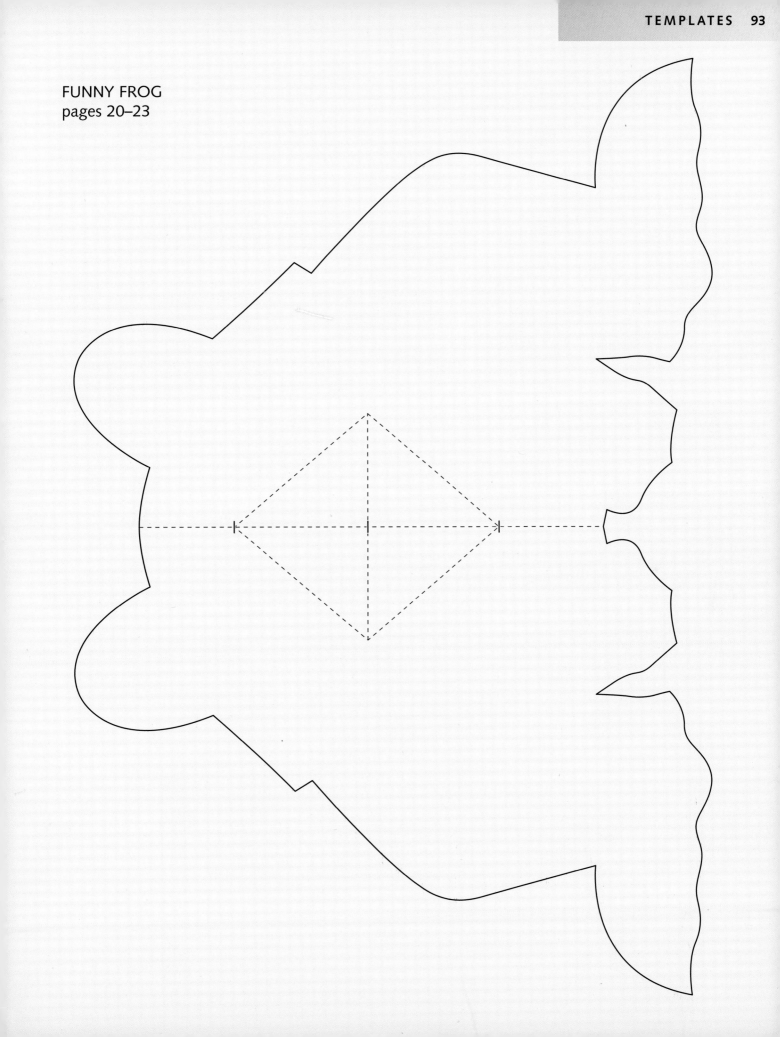

FUNNY FROG
pages 20–23

FUNNY FROG
pages 20–23

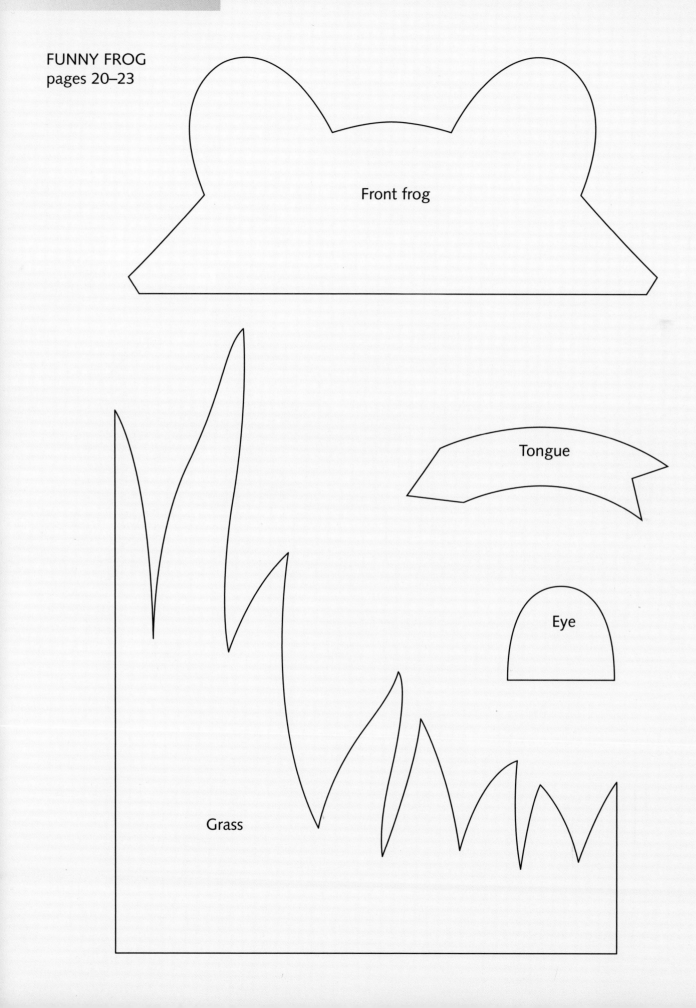

Front frog

Tongue

Eye

Grass

NEW HOME
pages 24–7

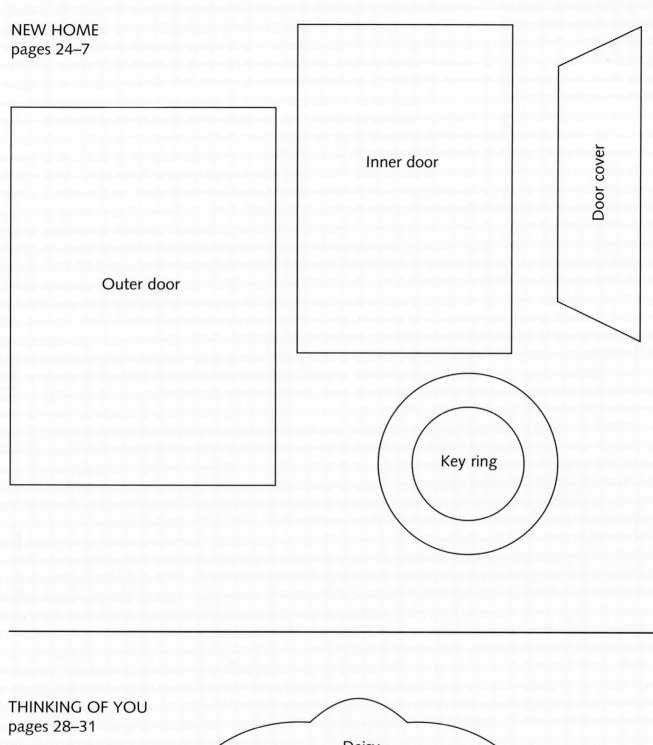

Outer door

Inner door

Door cover

Key ring

THINKING OF YOU
pages 28–31

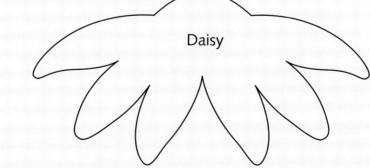

Daisy

GET WELL SOON
pages 32–5

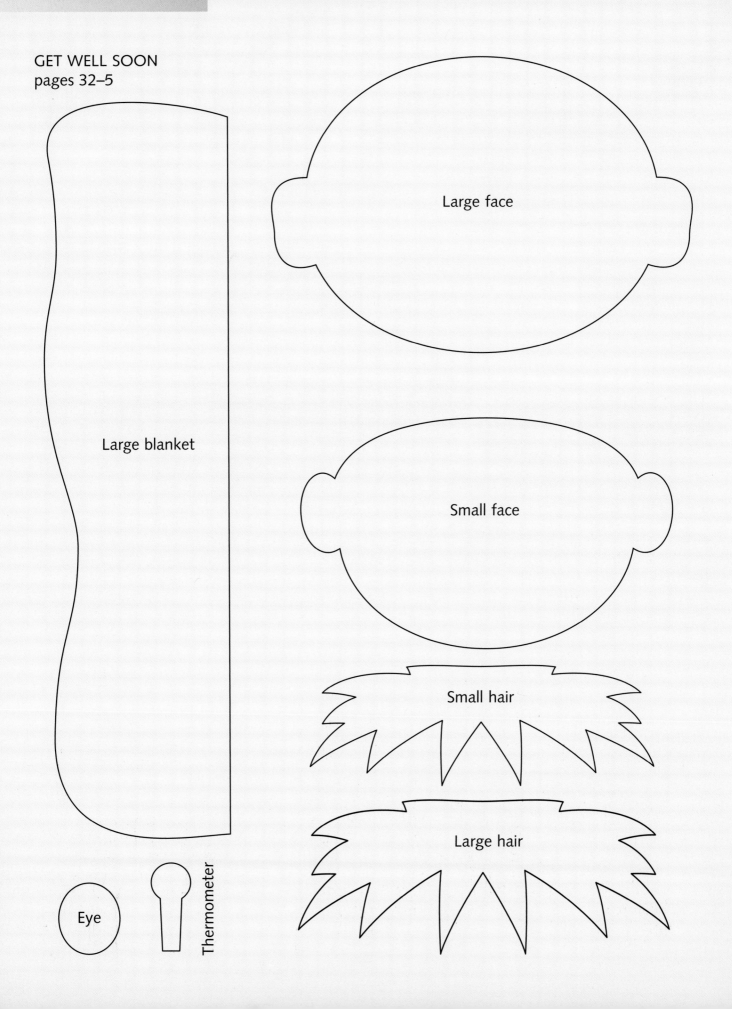

Large blanket

Large face

Small face

Small hair

Large hair

Eye

Thermometer

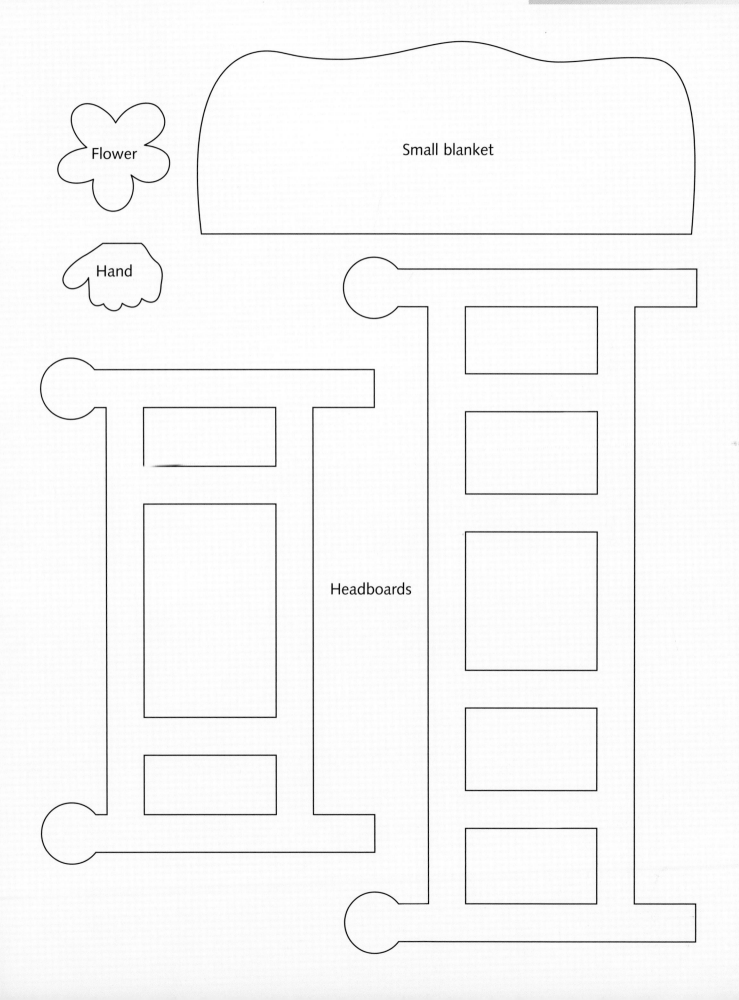

Flower

Small blanket

Hand

Headboards

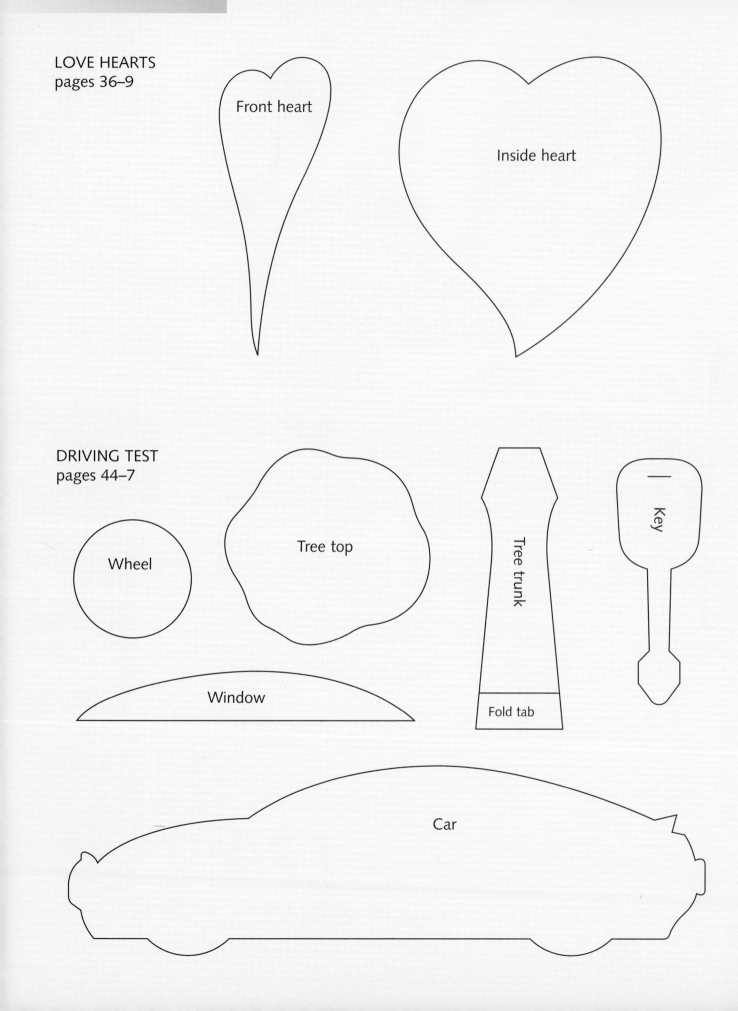

LOVE HEARTS
pages 36–9

Front heart

Inside heart

DRIVING TEST
pages 44–7

Wheel

Tree top

Tree trunk

Key

Window

Fold tab

Car

ALL TIED UP
pages 40–3

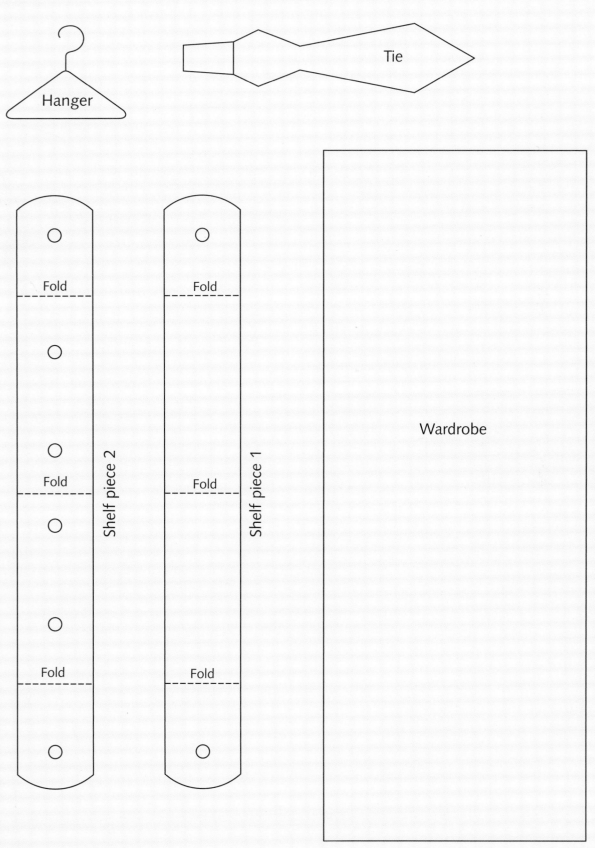

Hanger

Tie

Fold

Fold

Fold

Fold

Fold

Fold

Shelf piece 2

Shelf piece 1

Wardrobe

EASTER CHICK
pages 48–51

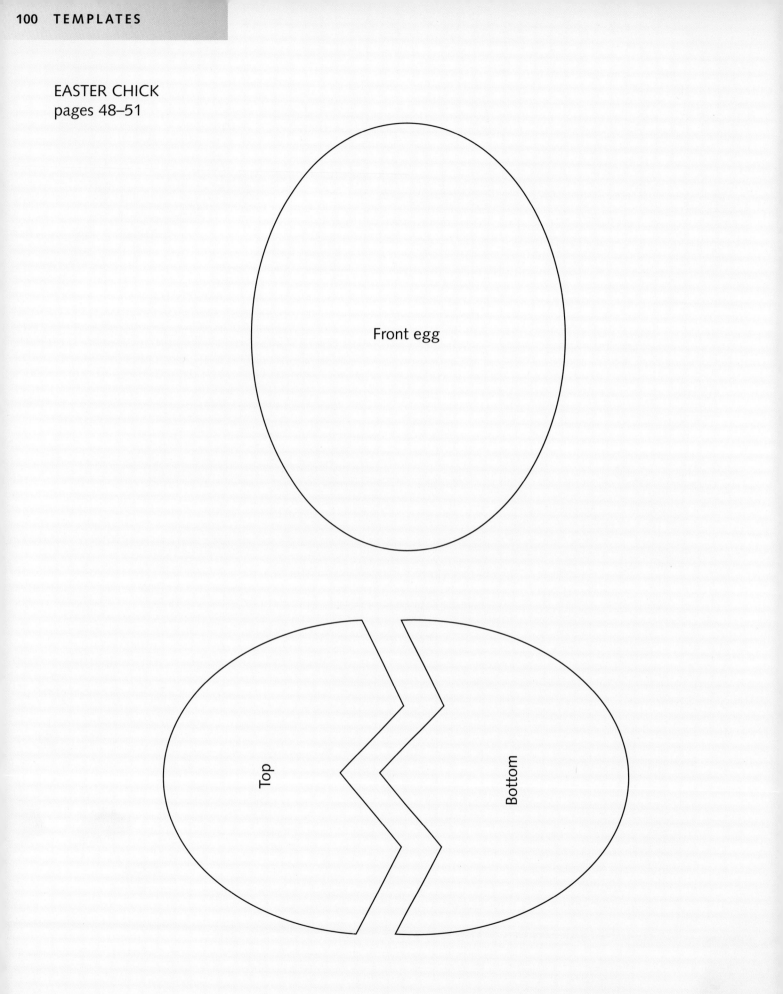

Front egg

Top

Bottom

EASTER CHICK
pages 48–51

Hair piece

Beak

Grass

Inside egg

Chick body

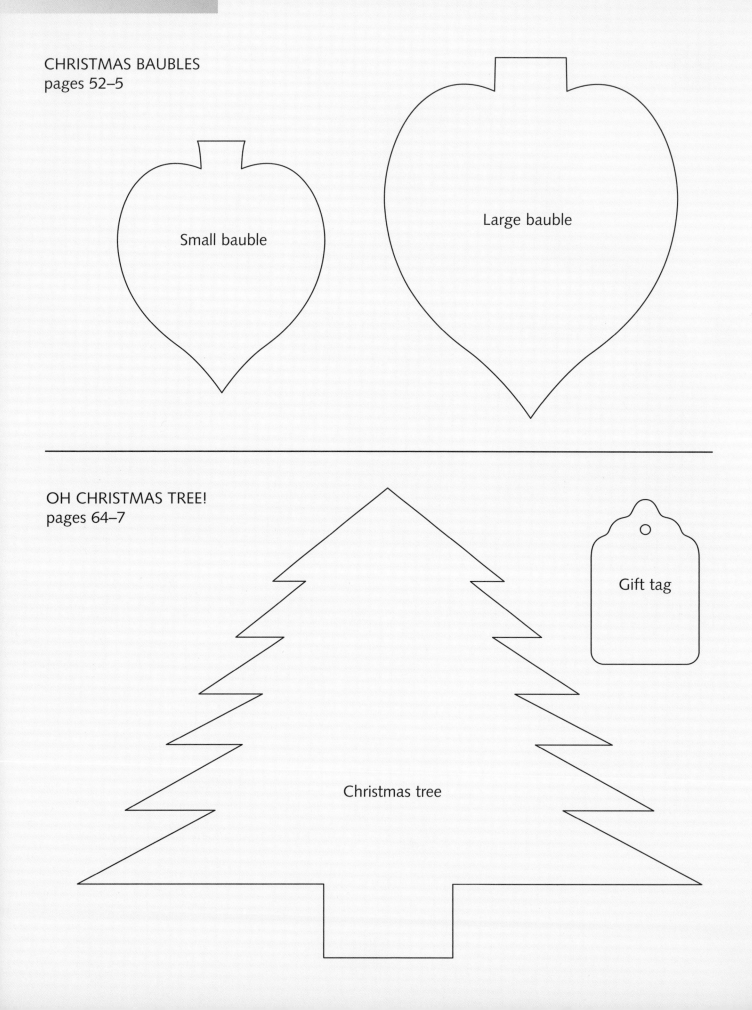

CHRISTMAS BAUBLES
pages 52–5

Small bauble

Large bauble

OH CHRISTMAS TREE!
pages 64–7

Gift tag

Christmas tree

SHOWER OF GIFTS
pages 56–9

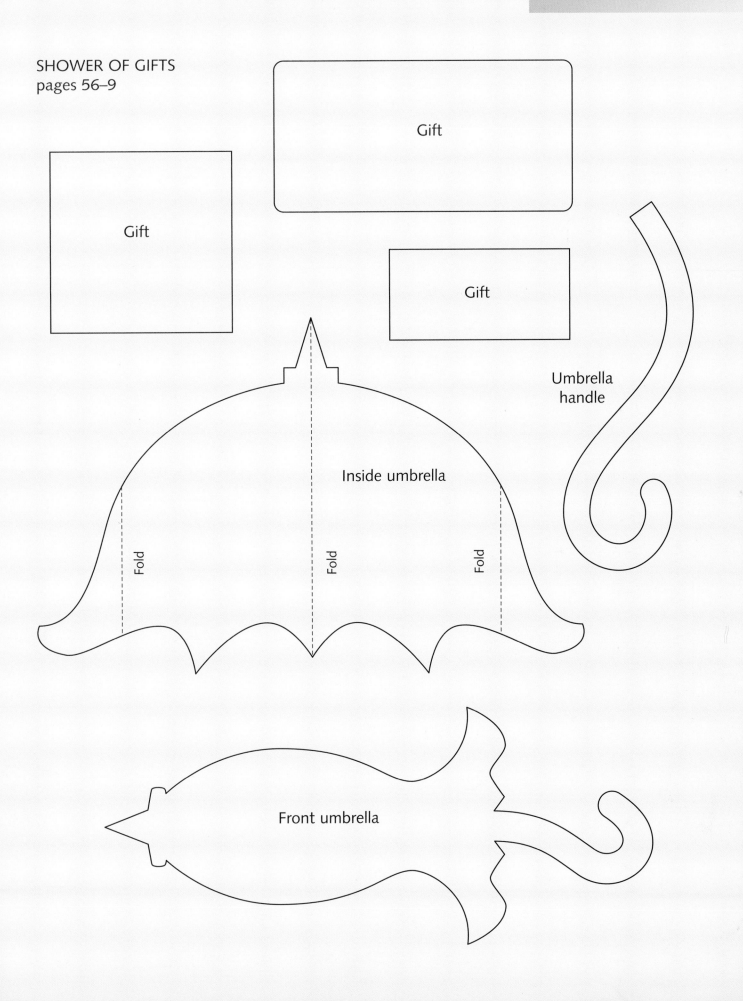

Gift

Gift

Gift

Umbrella
handle

Inside umbrella

Fold

Fold

Fold

Front umbrella

GREAT NEWS
pages 60–3

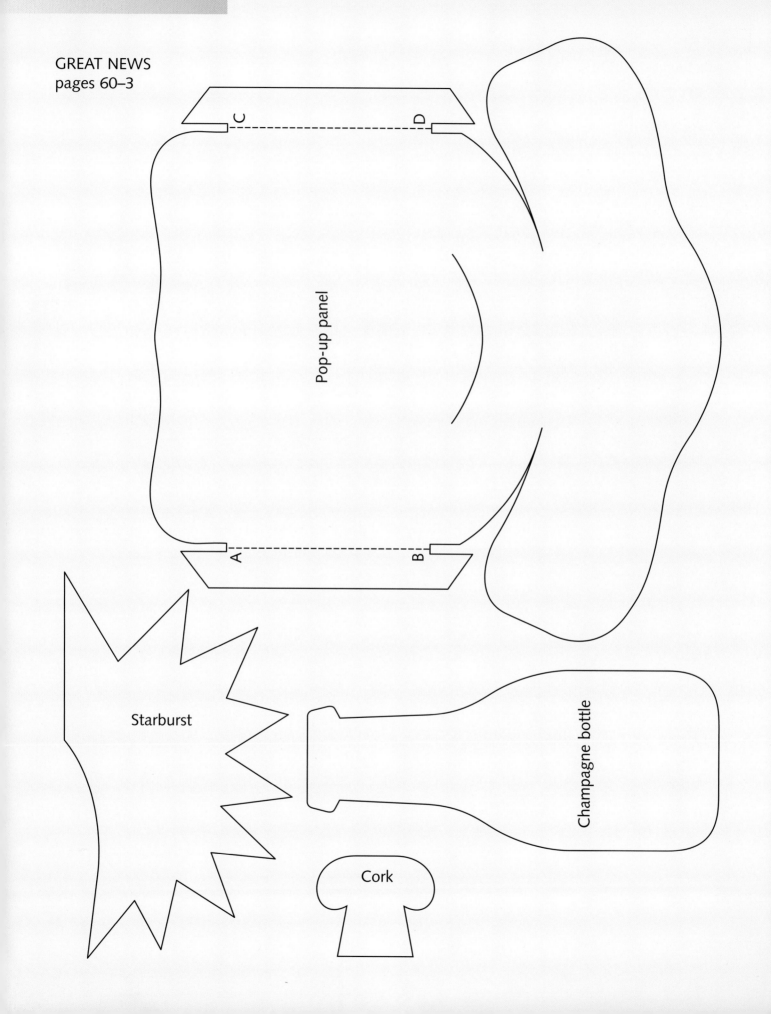

Pop-up panel

C   D

A   B

Starburst

Champagne bottle

Cork

BIRTHDAY SURPRISE
pages 68–71

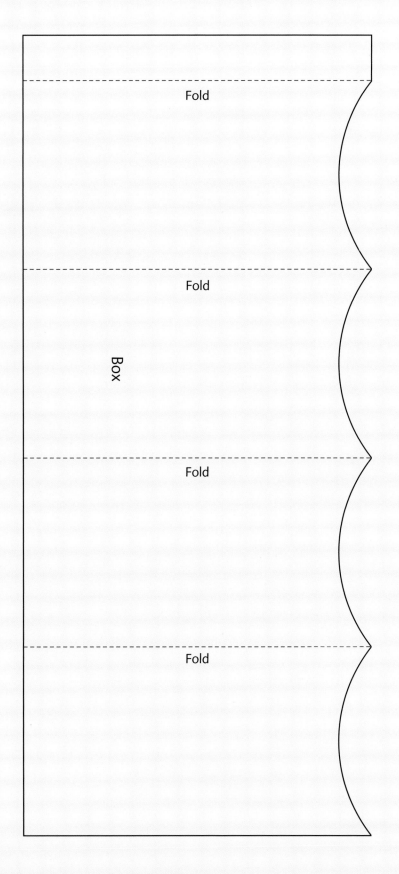

Fold

Fold

Box

Fold

Fold

BIRTHDAY SURPRISE
pages 68–71

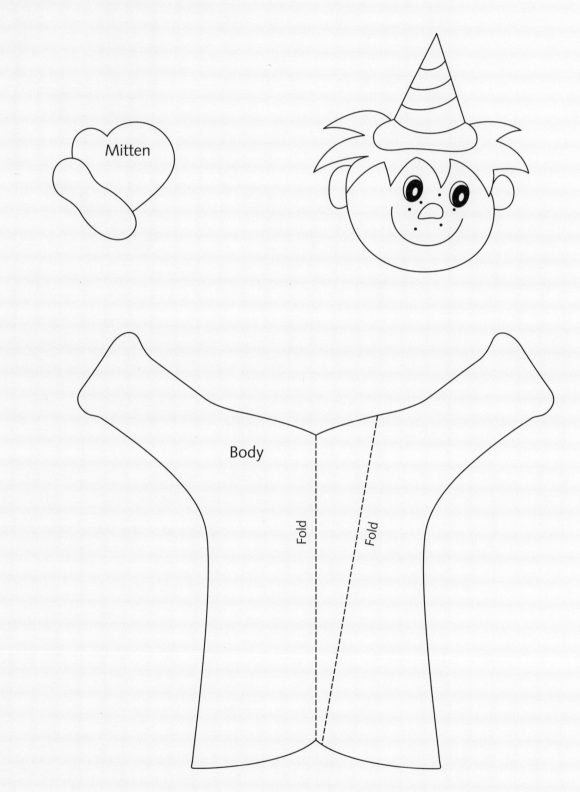

Mitten

Body

Fold

Fold

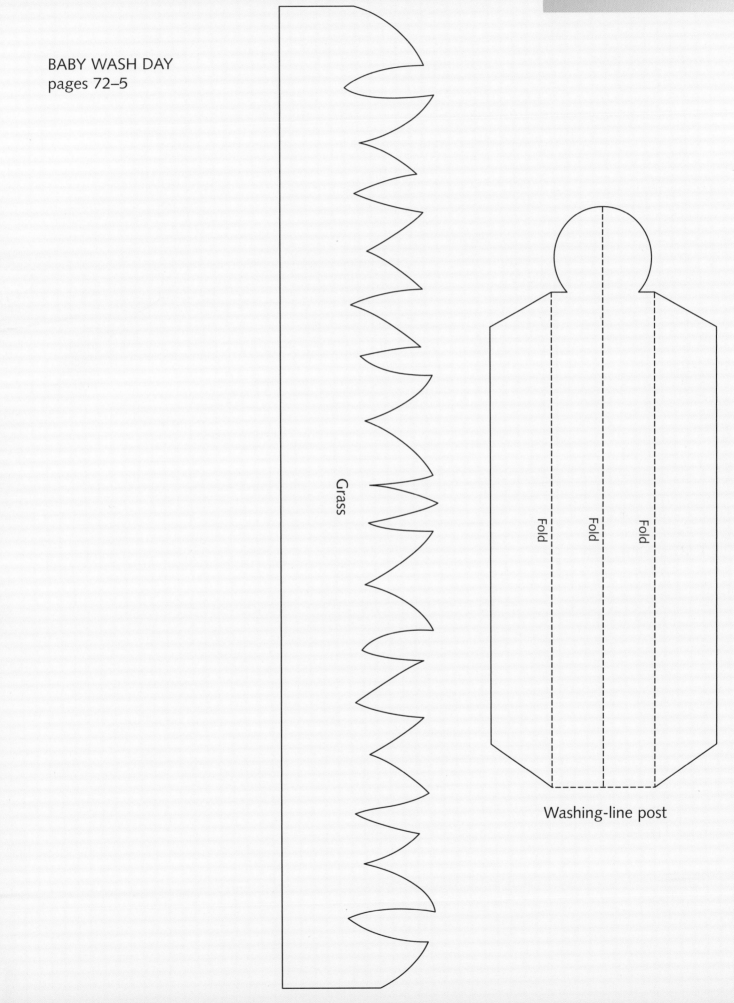

BABY WASH DAY
pages 72–5

Grass

Fold

Fold

Fold

Washing-line post

BABY WASH DAY
pages 72–5

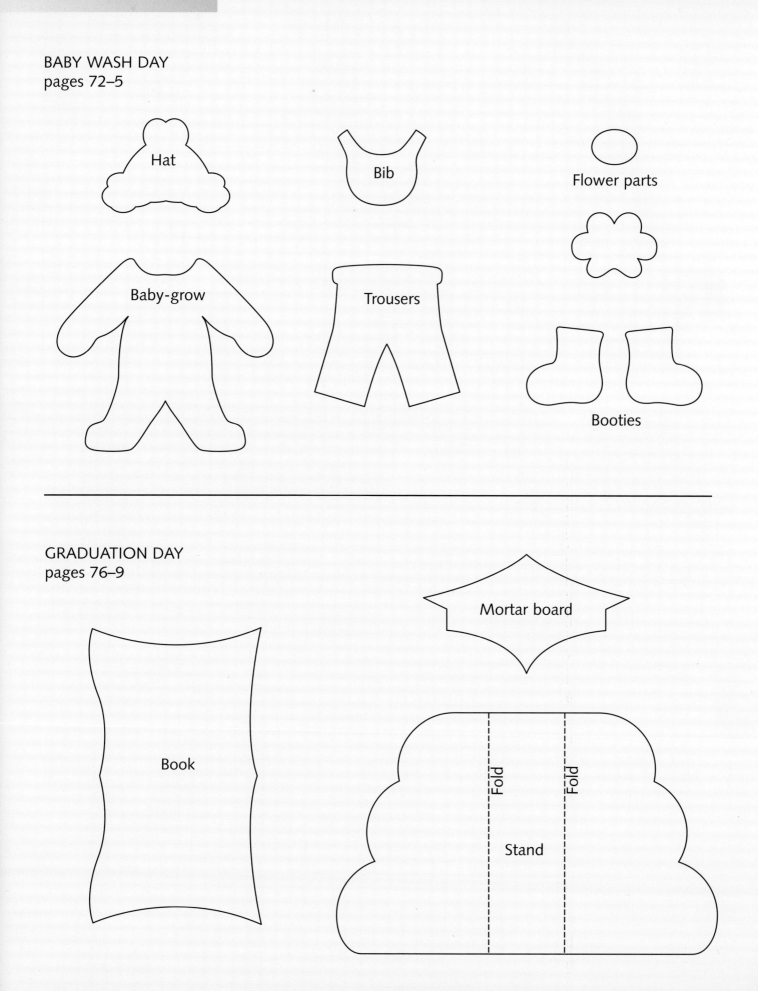

Hat

Bib

Flower parts

Baby-grow

Trousers

Booties

GRADUATION DAY
pages 76–9

Mortar board

Book

Fold

Fold

Stand

GRADUATION DAY
pages 76–9

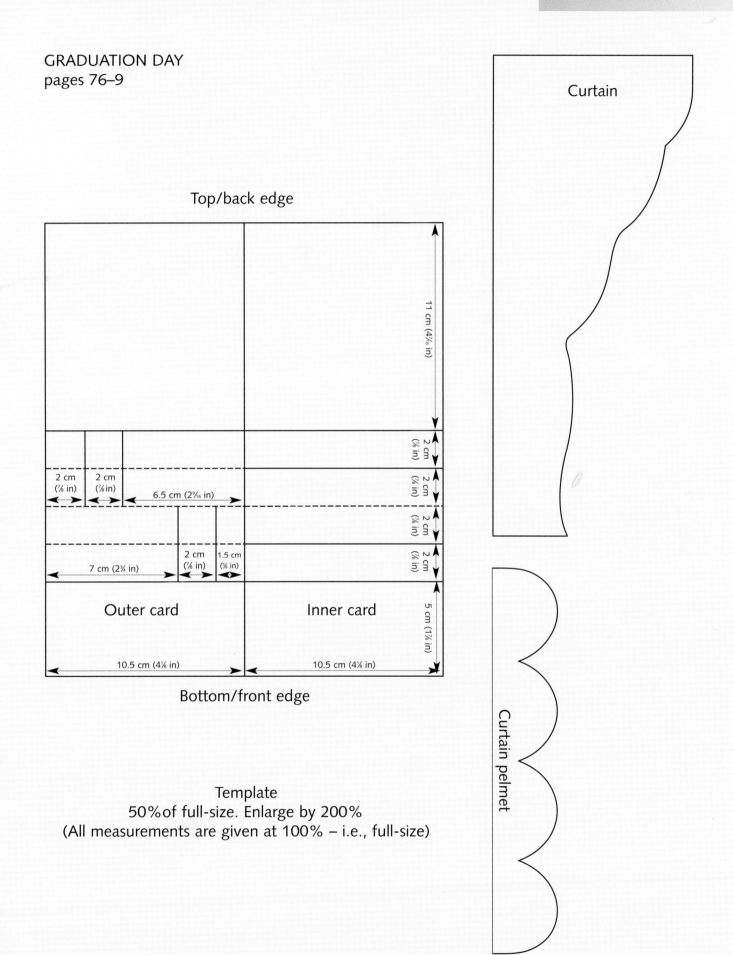

Top/back edge

11 cm (4⁵⁄₁₆ in)

2 cm (⅞ in)

2 cm (⅞ in)

2 cm (⅞ in)

6.5 cm (2⁹⁄₁₆ in)

2 cm (⅞ in)

2 cm (⅞ in)

2 cm (⅞ in)

1.5 cm (⅝ in)

7 cm (2¾ in)

5 cm (1⅞ in)

Outer card

Inner card

10.5 cm (4⅛ in)

10.5 cm (4⅛ in)

Bottom/front edge

Curtain

Curtain pelmet

Template
50% of full-size. Enlarge by 200%
(All measurements are given at 100% – i.e., full-size)

GOLDEN WEDDING BOWS
pages 80–3

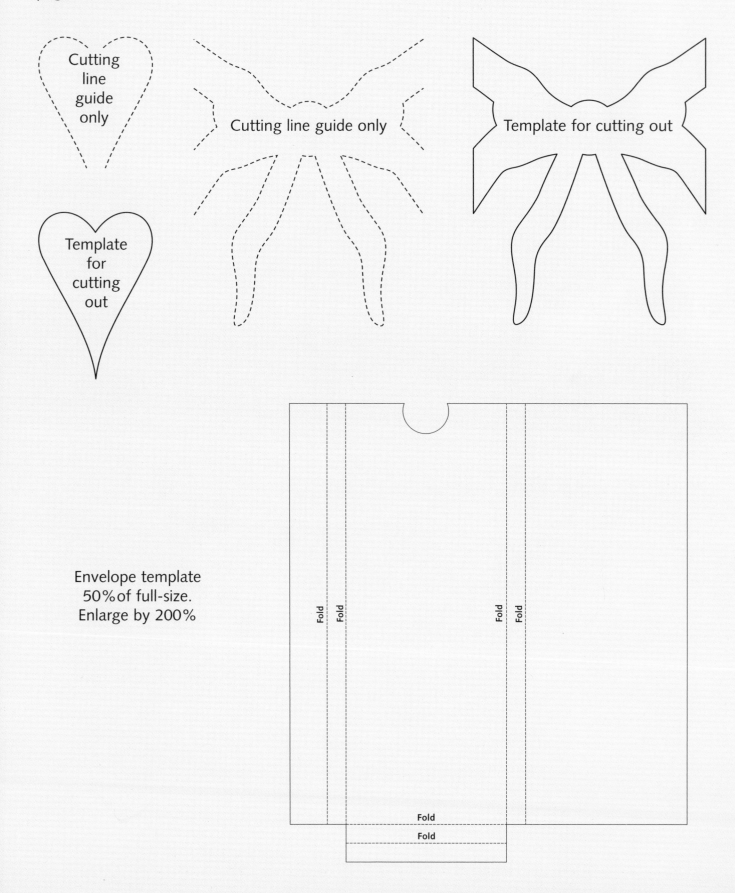

Cutting
line
guide
only

Template
for
cutting
out

Cutting line guide only

Template for cutting out

Envelope template
50% of full-size.
Enlarge by 200%

Fold

Fold

Fold

Fold

Fold

Fold

TIME TO SOW
pages 88–91

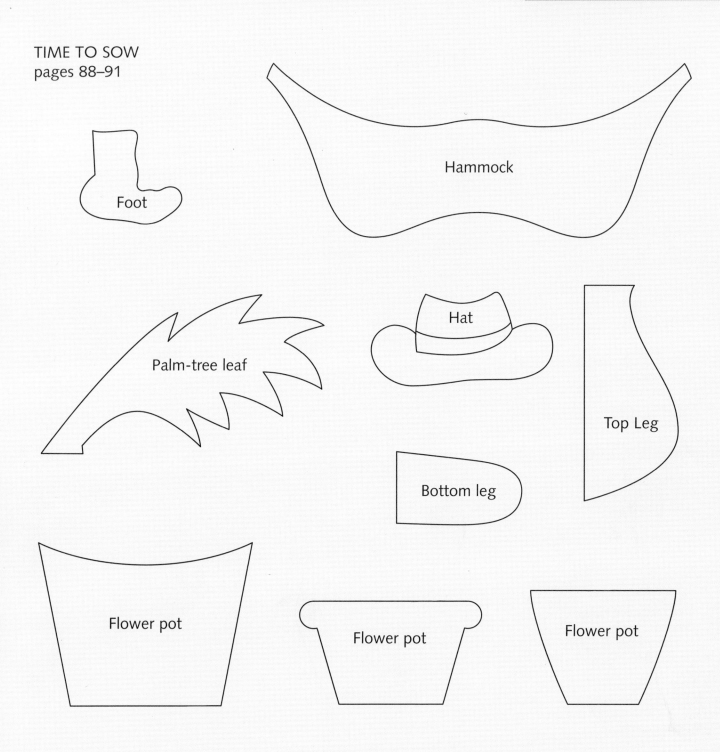

Foot

Hammock

Palm-tree leaf

Hat

Top Leg

Bottom leg

Flower pot

Flower pot

Flower pot

Fold

Fold

Tree trunk

Fold

Fold

Suppliers
Check the websites of these craft suppliers for stores in your area. Most offer a mail-order service, many internationally. A basic web search will throw up dozens more suppliers to try!

UK
Stamps
General craft supplier
www.stamps.co.uk

The Stamp Bug
Wide range of materials
www.thestampbug.co.uk

Elizybells Arts Stamps Ltd
Art and craft supplies
www.elzybells.co.uk

Fat Freddies Craft Shed
Wide range of cardmaking materials
Tel: 01904 799900

USA and Canada
Art Supply Warehouse
Art and craft supplies
www.aswexpress.com

Fiskars Brands, Inc.
General craft materials and tools
www.fiskars.com

Stampendous, Inc.
Rubber stamps
www.stampendous.com

South Africa
Arts, Crafts and Hobbies
General supplier
72 Hibernia Street, George 6529
Tel: 044 874 1337

Crafty Supplies
Shop UG 2, Stadium on Main, Main Road, Claremont 7700, Cape Town
Tel: 021 671 0286

Australia and New Zealand
LIncraft
General craft supplier. Stores throughout Australia
www.lincraft.com.au

Fine Art Papers
Artist materials and special papers
200 Madras Street, Christchurch, NZ
Tel: 03 379 4410

Index